GODDESS
on the GO

30 DAYS OF LOVE
SLOW DOWN & POUR INTO YOU

✳

LEORA EDUT

GODDESS
on the GO

Credits

DESIGN BY: LeAnna Weller Smith, www.wellersmithdesign.com

Copyright © 2021 Leora Edut
All rights reserved.
Reproduction without permission is strictly prohibited.

ISBN-13: 978-0-578-93132-6

DEDICATION

I dedicate this journal first to my daughter, who is the fire (Aries girl) that reminds me that if I could create life, everything else is a piece of cake. A special thanks to my "Oon," who is no longer here but was always a role model to follow my heart even if that didn't make sense to anyone else. Rounds and rounds of love to everyone who has ever supported the "Goddess on the Go" movement – if it wasn't for you, we would not be here.

CONTENTS

Introduction 7

What is Self-Love? with Tiff 10

Morning Love with Leora Edut 14

Family Constellation Self-Love Ritual with Leora Edut 17

Cultivating Self-Love with Yvonna Kopacz 20

Flirting Is for You! with Janna 22

Reset Your Life Ritual with Abiola Abrams 25

Orgasmic Manifestation with Anita Kopacz 28

Loving the Luxurious Skin You're In
    with Bernadette Pleasant 31

Self-Love Ritual with Chef Ameera 34

Self-Pleasure Ritual with Devi Maisha 36

Crystals into Self-Love with Dinan Ra 38

Self-Love Ritualsss! With Jameelah Assata Auset 40

Hello Ritual with Karla Lightfoot 43

Ritual of Everyday Feng Shui with Kate Mackinnon 46

Self-Love... Deep Breath with Kathleen Booker 48

Self-Love Journal with Kimberly Simms 50

I Am Ritual with Krystal Athena Hubbard 54

What Does Your Self-Love Look Like Today?
    with Lauren Harkness 55

Inner Teen Self-Love Ritual with Laurena Brittain 57

CPR Method with Lotus Laloba 63

Crystals for Self-Love with Mercedes 66

Astrostyle Summer Solstice Ritual with Ophira & Tali Edut 69

Creating Space Ritual with Monica Shah 74

Yoni Steam Ritual with Alicia Hudson 76

Circle of Power with Shannon Carson 78

Breathe into Body Love with Tania Sterly 80

Self-Value and Money with Rhonda 83

Listening to Our Intuitive Knowing is Self-Love
    with Vanessa C. Codorniu 86

Self-Love Ritual with Xtina 89

Vision Ritual with Yadi Alba 93

Shama Self-Love with Shama Dhanani 96

A Self-Care Ritual to Fall in Love with You
    with Gigi Robinson 98

30 Days of Love

SLOW DOWN & POUR INTO YOU

Divinely Collected by
LEORA EDUT

Introduction

SELF-LOVE IS NOT A ONE STOP DESTINATION, INSTEAD, IT'S A MOMENT TO MOMENT CHOICE to choose yourself. It can at times feel as if we are unraveling if we have always put others needs before our own. If we have spent our lives watching our mothers, grandmothers, and aunties ignore the call of slowing down, it's hard to break ourselves from these loyalties. We all want a quick fix but self-love is until we take our last breath.

Spending the first part of my life nurturing everyone else I had learned to be the savior and played the victim role well too. At 27 I was suffering from exhaustion, emotionally eating to fill the void, and dating anyone who asked me out because I thought love existed outside of myself.

Discovering self-love at age 32 felt foreign to me and it certainly wasn't an overnight process. Choosing to stop drinking alcohol, as a reason to numb out the parts of myself that felt anxious when I went out to social events, was the start. Seeing Leora was pretty dope just by being herself felt soooo good. Wanting to be present to experience the fullness of life was the start as well as the desire to connect with others authentically were new ways to love myself.

Honoring my time became another way I up-leveled my relationship with myself. My money coach once had me do a chart on time I had to look at who and what I was giving my time too. When I looked deeply I was spending 90% of my time obsessing about an ex where the relationship was not moving in a healthy direction for either one of us. Valuing who and what I said yes to become another lesson on the pathway.

Traveling felt like a thing rich people do. Growing up we went out on 3 family vacations 2 of which I think my grandparents helped with. I could somehow come up with money for other things yet coming up with money to travel somewhere I had always dreamed of felt like too much. Waiting for someone else to swoop me away to some getaway wasn't happening. My girlfriends wanted to go to Costa Rica. How could I say no? There was such a strong desire to have that experience with them that the energy of YES I am going to pull the money in. From that day on I have not stopped traveling. Spending time with Mother Earth whether it be mountains, oceans, green lush acres of grass flirting in between my toes, the trees whispering wisdom as I walk past each one. Outside of my own 4 walls I see parts of myself I could not discover being in that familiar space.

Becoming a mom was one of the most difficult destinations along the way. Feeling as if I could not physically put myself in front of a tiny human who depended on me for survival, finding time to hear myself in silence became a thing of the past for a while. I will never forget.

When my daughter was 6 months old, I had an opportunity to go overnight for a getaway with my girlfriends. Needing this like nobody's business I felt guilty about leaving my baby girl at home with her dad. Feeling extremely anxious about being away from my baby for the first time I struggled for about 90 minutes before I chose myself. After that night I realized how many moms never return to themselves even after their children become older. Reclaiming our lives is necessary to break the cycles of women dying of stress and checkout.

Choosing relationships where I was fed, being seen without judgement, and held in my most vulnerable moments was another meeting point on the map of self-love. Releasing the obligation to remain in relationships because of history or worry of what people would say about you changing your circle is not enough of a good reason to stay. Picking people who make you feel good about yourself, something about that gives more breath to my body. Repeat after me "boundaries serve me" and "joy is my birthright

Loving ourselves is a unique experience and many of us forget to practice it consistently. I've certainly fallen off many moments along the way. If it wasn't for my own community of womxn around me teaching me, lovingly given me some truth serum about when I wasn't speaking up for myself, times I was putting too much pressure on myself to push through a timeline or be a "perfect person" I would not embody this whole self-love thing. That is why I created *Goddess On The Go- 30 Days Of Love – Slow Down & Pour Into You.*

> "
> LOVING OURSELVES IS A UNIQUE EXPERIENCE AND MANY OF US FORGET TO PRACTICE IT CONSISTENTLY. I'VE CERTAINLY FALLEN OFF MANY MOMENTS ALONG THE WAY.

What Is Self-Love?

TIFF GODDESS LIFE OF A GODDESS

What is Self-Love?

Is it loving the way you look? Is it treating yourself with the finer things? It is doing what makes you feel happy? I mean, I've always thought I had self-love until I realized it is so much deeper than a pretty face, treating myself with the finer things or doing what "makes" me happy. Are you doing what really makes you happy? Sooo, are you?

See, self-love is what we all think we have figured out but, we misunderstand the importance of it. It's not our fault though. The good thing is we have control over it, and it's never too late to love yourself.

SELF–LOVE IS REACHING OUT FOR THAT ONE THING THAT'LL SET YOUR SOUL FREE.

It's admitting that you truly need to love yourself a lot more than you thought you were. Self-love is accepting change and understanding that you have control over everything that comes your way. Self-love is knowing that everything you need is within you and ensuring that you are loving yourself on all levels mentally, physically and emotionally.

Self-love is taking the time out for ourselves to heal parts of us that we didn't love the most. It's being able to recognize what's not right for us so that we can work towards being a better version of ourselves. Self-love is looking in the mirror and knowing that you deserve better so you will do anything in your power to make sure of it.

Self-love is shedding tears but also being strong enough to wipe them away and keep right on loving yourself. Self-love is letting go of the old and allowing new things to come. It's expressing how you feel and not caring what others think about it. Self-love is surrounding yourself with positive energy wanting to protect every part of who you're becoming.

Self-love is creating a life you want and realizing your worth. Self-love is being patient with yourself and embracing the journey of every phase that you go through. Self-love is forgiving ourselves and others so that we can take the next step in our lives. Self-love is losing it all and gaining it right back despite the difficulties. Self-love is taking control over our negative thoughts and replacing them with positive ones.

Self-love is understanding that before you can truly love or make someone else happy, you have to love yourself first. Self-love is staying consistent with yourself and your goals. Self-love is nourishing your mind, body, and soul. Self-love is everything you should be doing right now for you. So, think about it. Are you taking the time out to love you? If not, start today. I'll start right along with you because everyday is a perfect day to love yourself all over again.

Here are 20 self-love affirmations to power up that self-love.

1. I believe in myself

2. I am free of worry and at peace with who I am

3. I am in love with myself

4. I choose to be positive

5. I am proud of myself and all that I have accomplished

6. I allow myself to change for the better

7. I trust my healing journey

8. I am beautiful

9. I trust that I am ready to transform into my higher self

10. I speak how I feel, I openly expressive myself

11. I make my own decisions, it's okay to say no.

12. What I give is what I receive

13. I am not broken

14. I am free from past hurt

15. I love the body that I am in

16. I choose to be happy and love myself to the fullest today

17. I am proud of myself and all that I have accomplished

18. I am now creating a life I want to live

19. All I need is self love

20. I get better and better everyday

"But after I state the affirmations, what should I do next"? is a question I used to ask too, but don't worry, I got you.

Practicing self-love — 5 tips:

1 Find Your Tribe.
Surround yourself with people who love and support you through everything that you intend to do. Great energy is a good source of self-love, so make sure you surround yourself with positive, uplifting people.

2 Do What You Love.
It is nothing better than doing what you love to do no matter what others feel. Grow with it and allow it to flow while loving yourself.

3 Be Mindful Of What You Eat.
When we eat good, we feel good. That's the first step of taking care of our mind, body, and soul. I'm not gonna say this anymore, lol, sike, I am but "we are what we eat".

4 Challenge Yourself.
Set a goal. Do something different. Lessons come from the most uncomfortable places.

5 Say What You Feel.
There's no better feeling than to say how you feel. Never hold back. When you are being open and honest to others, you are being honest with yourself.

6 Yoga All D*** Day
I mean, I don't literally mean all day, but yoga is a great way to practice self-love. It opens your heart to new things and gives you feeling to just flow. So take the time out to do some yoga. Start slow stretches help too.

7 Meditate
Meditating was a challenge for me because I truly had to focus. You can shift your mind by just focusing on all positive things in your life. You can state affirmations while meditating, state the things you love about yourself and what you are grateful for. This is how I'll meditate, but do what works for you. Just find a comfy, quiet spot and focus on you.

LOVE YOU, TIF

ABOUT TIF

I am honored to adorn you in my beautiful creations, guide you on your path to connect with your inner soul, and help you manifest your dream life! I'm a multidimensional spiritual being on her journey and is a beautiful light to those on theirs. Let's start discovering who you truly are

Instagram: @lifeofagoddess.1111

Morning Love

LEORA EDUT, GODDESS ON THE GO

THE MOMENT WE RISE, BEFORE WE START FEELING THAT PULL TO TAKE CARE OF THE WORLD, IT'S SO IMPORTANT WE LAND IN OUR OWN BODIES FIRST. Over the years, my morning rituals have varied from 3 hours (pre-mom, family) to 45 minutes. Sometimes I have to do a modified version in 20 minutes when I have a tight timeline, but regardless, it is rare that I miss a day.

Having a consistent space to come to makes all the difference. This is your sacred place in your home where you can fill it up with your own energy. I love to energize my space with crystals, fresh flowers, art, candles, journals, cards to pull, oils, sprays etc. In the center of the space is where you want to place all of your delicious items so you can be reminded that surrounding yourself in beauty is the lifestyle you are pu$$afesting daily. (P.S. we do not manifest; we pu$$afest because all of our magic comes from the place we give birth.)

Begin your day by lighting a candle signifying a new moment in your life. Light some sage to clear away any stress or worry that you may have woken with. Breathe in the scents, take 10 full-bodied breaths in, feel each ounce of that unnecessary energy leaving your gorgeous temple as you exhale.

Turn on a meditation for at least 10 minutes - some of my faves you can find on YouTube or Spotify are Abiola Abrams and Deepak Chopra – and focus on an area you want to work on in your life. Maybe it's opening your heart to receive more love or attracting the abundance you desire. Nothing happens overnight, so choose something you want to really focus your attention on for at least 30-90 days.

HAVING A CONSISTENT SPACE TO COME TO MAKES ALL THE DIFFERENCE..

After meditation, it's time to wake the body up. You'll want to have a yoga mat or some soft comfy pillow for this – at least 3 so they can hold the length of your body. I love to start with something sloooowww like "Waterloo" by JONES. As you lay on your mat, let the sounds of the song come into your body before you move an inch. Close your eyes. Notice how the music makes your body feel. Ask your body which part wants to move? Maybe you want to roll your wrists around or stretch your arms and legs like you are gently reaching for the morning sun. Your body could desire to roll around on the floor, feeling the cool earth underneath you and reminding you that you are always held. Do this for the entire song, allowing yourself to truly relish in the gifts of pouring into yourself.

Once that song ends, get into a seating position. Play the next song – "The Zone" by The Weekend and Drake – and let your hands begin to explore the places you normally avoid. Continue to keep your eyes closed to take in the inner wisdom and pleasure you are experiencing. Massage the back of your neck, do some slow sitting hip circles, stirring that feminine energy up, go into some downward dogs and child poses to allow more life-force energy to flow from the top of your head to the bottom of your feet.

Eventually, come up to a standing position. What song brings you joy? Turn that on and let your body skip, spin around in circles, jump up and down, anything that reminds you that your inner child loves it when you give them attention.

Once you have had your time on the dance floor, it's time to take that energy and seal in your desires. I love having several decks of angel or tarot cards here. Feel which deck your intuition is pulling you towards. Morning messages that we receive outside of our very loud morning doomsday voices are so helpful. Pull at least 3-5 cards here. I recommend The Moon Deck and The Goddess Decks – they are awesome!

Take out your journal and begin free writing. Do not judge what comes up. All emotions are good emotions. You may be inspired by some of the messages you received. I love to start my journal with "Dear Angels, Ancestors, and Guides." Always make sure to ask for what you want, whether it's to send more love throughout our planet, to pu$$afest large lump sums of unexpected money, or a desired opportunity that seems far out of your reach. There is something beyond our linear mind that exists when we write it down. Put it out there, and trust that having the desire is enough for us to magnetize it our way.

Give thanks to yourself for taking the time out to nurture and be compassionate with yourself. Offer the altar an item of gratitude for all that it holds for us, whether it's putting rose petals or flowers on for love, several dollar bills to call in more abundance, or a picture of an ancestor(s) to assist with healing.

Family Constellation Self-Love Ritual

LEORA EDUT, GODDESS ON THE GO

FOR MANY OF US, WE WATCHED OUR MOTHERS AND GRANDMOTHERS FORGET ABOUT THEMSELVES. Whether the times they were in were different from those we live in, or they experienced loss or unhealed trauma from their ancestors. Many of us come from grandparents or great grandparents that were impacted by times of war, slavery, the Holocaust, Jim Crow era, poverty/survival. We also may have experienced adoption, abuse, loss of a sibling, parent abandonment, or a loss of a parent at a young age. Where did self-love even fit in or have a right to have a place?

THE TRUTH IS OUR ANCESTORS DO NOT WANT US TO SUFFER IN THE WAYS THAT THEY DID, EVEN IF THEY NEVER HAVE THE TOOLS TO TELL US THAT THEMSELVES IN OUR LIFETIME. We are going to work with the tools of Family Constellation today. A constellation may sound like it has something to do with astrology, but it is actually our family's combined energetic system that is passed down to us. When we are born, it comes through us and often stands in front of us as an impossible block. Clearing this energy can help us receive the support of our ancestors and allow us to move forward differently than in the ways they were able to.

CLOSE YOUR EYES AND CALL IN THE SUPPORT OF YOUR ANCESTORS BEHIND YOU. Your father on your right shoulder and your mom on your left shoulder. No matter what kind of relationship you had with them, energetically, they are your parents, and you are their kid. Take in 3 long, deep inhales here. See if you can breathe in even more support from them.

Now, see yourself in a large empty room that you know the layout of really well and see the energy of self-love come in. Turn towards your mother and father and say to them, "Dear parents, it's been really hard to find parts of my worth in the world, and I often don't ask for help when I need it most. I'm asking for your blessing to surpass you in receiving love and support in my life, not in betrayal of you but in honor of you."

Then, take a deep, cleansing breath. Hear your parents speak your name: "Dear _____, you have our blessing to go forth and welcome all the love and care you need in honor of us." Take a deep breath and allow yourself to truly receive this blessing.

Feel yourself turn and face forward and see self-love in front of you. Tell that self-love, "I see you, and I wasn't ready for you before, but in this moment, I am fully ready to have you be a part of my life."

Hear self-love say to you, "It's really good to see you, I'm so happy you chose me." Take another deep breath and if it's okay, allow self-love to give you a hug, and if you would like to, you can give-self-love a hug. Take this moment and put it in a picture frame in your heart, seal it here and now that it will be with you whenever you need it.

Come out from this meditative state, give your body a good shakeout, and journal anything that came up - no judgment here. Place a pillow behind yourself for the next 30 days and let that pillow represent self-love. Lean into it and feel it supporting you from behind. Pick up a rose quartz stone from the crystal store small enough to keep in your left pocket, which is the side of your heart chamber. Keep it there for 30 or more days and let it assist you in supporting you with more self-love in your life.

THE TRUTH IS OUR ANCESTORS DO NOT WANT US TO SUFFER IN THE WAYS THAT THEY DID, WVWN IF THEY NEVER HAVE THE TOOLS TO TELL US THAT THEMSELVES IN OUR LIFETIME

ABOUT LEORA

How it All Began:

After struggling with depression, unfulfillment, and desperation to feel a sense of pleasure and connection, Leora created Goddess on the Go in 2012. These live weekend events brought women together globally to embody all layers of their divinity, from sensuality to sadness. In 2018, Leora authored the book <u>Goddess on the Go: Rituals to Help You Slow Down and Slay</u> in 2018 (Available at Barnes and Noble and Amazon). Becoming certified in Family Constellation Therapy as well as becoming a Femme! attuned teacher, Leora supports her clients in healing ancestral trauma and unprocessed stored emotions through somatic experience. She has been featured in numerous publications including Elle magazine, Lucky magazine, the New York Post and the LA Times. A dynamic public speaker, she has appeared on stage with Marianne Williamson and has been a guest on the Dr Oz show. Committed to activism, she sits on the board for The Power of You Teens, an organization in Harlem that empowers young women at risk with self-love, entrepreneurship, and creating a vision to step into.

Instagram @goddessonthego1

Cultivating Self-Love

WITH YVONNA KOPACZ

A Bath Ritual

So, I have several go-to self-love rituals that I have cultivated over the years. A daily bath complete with my Lomar Farms candle and bath salts, a body-oil rub down, making sure I thank every beautiful bump and curve, followed by a sweet midday nap that resets most if not all of the tensions accumulated throughout the day. You see, I'm one of those high achieving, control lovers that takes even my self-care practices very seriously. But that wasn't always the case.

Self-Care Practice

Being a mother, a wife, an owner of my own business, there wasn't any time left after caring for my brood to lavishly tend to any wants that I had. I thought it was more important to make sure everybody else's needs were met before mine. How could I possibly make time for myself when there wasn't enough time in the day to finish all the tasks on my list? It was only when I was close to a breakdown that I realized that a self-love routine should be my priority and that EVERYONE reaped the benefit when Mama was happy and loved up. So, now I make sure Yvonna is cared for even when life gets so full and "out of control."

Body Communication

I've also reached a point in my life that the connection I have cultivated with my body is now dictating how I love it up. Your body is always communicating with you. Our amazing vessels hold the imprint of scars and traumas as well as all the good that has happened. Our bodies are highly capable of letting us know what it needs at any time if we just take the time to listen. Sitting for a short quiet meditation, taking walks in nature, and taking time to stretch and move our bodies helps deepen the relationship to our bodies and ensures that we can connect to our needs and wants in the healthiest of ways. When stress and anxiety arises, take a deep breath and ask yourself what would be most helpful for you and your body.

YOU CAN ALWAYS STAY PRESENT WITH NEW AND UNIQUE WAYS TO SHOW LOVE TO YOURSELF.

ABOUT YVONNA

Best known for her eight-year tenure as Melissande Bauer on Guiding Light, Yvonna Kopacz Wright began her career as a model after entering a contest in Seventeen Magazine. Since then, she has appeared in various TV shows and movies, such as Cosby, Damages, Unforgettable, Perfect Stranger and more. Yvonna is also a beekeeper who is extremely passionate about educating others on the current situation of the honeybee, including what we can do to help keep them from extinction. She takes care of her own hives, volunteers at kids schools and community centers teaching the youth about the importance of bees in our ecosystem, and uses social media as a platform for spreading her knowledge. Yvonna recently turned her passion into a business by selling hand-made beautiful beeswax candles and other products from the bees, naming it Lomar Farms after her two beautiful daughters, Lola and Marley. Yvonna is also very dedicated to inspiring and uplifting women in her community and around the globe.

Instagram @yvonnakopaczwright @lomarfarms

Flirting Is For You!

WITH JANNA

ONE OF THE MOST IMPORTANT ASPECTS OF BURLESQUE IS EYE CONTACT WITH YOUR AUDIENCE. What makes a performance sexy is when the performer has the confidence to look you right in the eyes while they are performing.

THAT DIRECT EYE CONTACT MAKES THE AUDIENCE FEEL SEEN, ACKNOWLEDGED AND ENTHRALLED!

Let's play around with that idea, except we are going to look at ourselves through some fun mirror work. I'll admit that being face to face with ourselves in the mirror can feel very vulnerable, awkward and overwhelming. But it is important for us to be able to see the beauty in ourselves without needing external validation. Our divinity is calling for our attention!

Before we start, here's what you need:

1. 5-10 minutes of uninterrupted time

2. A mirror that you can get close to (can be handheld, a compact, on a wall, etc.)

3. A song that ymakes you feel juicy

Close your eyes and ground yourself by inhaling and exhaling deeply and slowly. Feel the floor beneath you holding you, and supporting you. Open your eyes and look in the mirror. Look directly in the reflection of your own eyes as if you'd look into the eyes of a lover. Say something sweet to yourself in the mirror out loud. It can be a familiar affirmation or something about yourself you've just noticed and admire.

Examples:

"I am a goddess inside and out."

"Damn, I'm fine!"

"My body is a blessing as it is today."

"I receive with ease."

"My lips are luscious and sexy."

"I trust myself."

REPEAT IT A TOTAL OF 3 TIMES. Now put on that juicy song and flirt with yourself in the mirror. Yes, you read that right. Put on the music and look at yourself in the mirror as you'd look at someone who turns you all the way on! Bat your eyelashes at yourself, wink, smile coyly, giggle, lick your lips. Do whatever feels good to acknowledge your own magic, sexiness and divinity. And if you feel silly, repeat your affirmation again to help you reconnect with your goddess reflection. Have fun, you deserve the best!

ABOUT JANNA

Jaz is an international burlesque teacher, performer and mixed media artist focused on supporting women and non-binary people in activating and accentuating their sensuality. Her performance style and choreography merges African diaspora dance forms including AfroCuban, Haitian, Congolese and hiphop with her studies of burlesque as a liberatory practice. Jaz teaches burlesque and sensual movement classes to people of all shades, shapes, sizes, abilities and gender expressions. She enjoys classes for groups, individuals, couples and anyone who is interested in loving up themselves!

Instagram @jannazinzi

Reset Your Life Ritual

WITH ABIOLA ABRAMS

Self-Renewal Blessing Ritual

Have you ever felt like you needed a reset? You have a right to start over at any time. If we are blessed to live long enough, there will be many times when we need to reset, restart, reboot and make a comeback.

Unfortunately, at times we feel pressured by every voice other than our own, beaten down by the systemic oppression of the patriarchy's last gasp and just plain drained.

You, my divine goddess sister, are a magical force of nature. You deserve to be happy, healthy, beautiful, rich, and turned on by your own life. You deserve to have the courage to stand up for what is right and be the person you were born to be.

Resetting ourselves with ritual aligns us with our ancestral power and reawakens the power of the divine within. I have had to restart after perceived failures, heartbreaks and miscarriages. I have needed a reboot when celebrating a new business or relationship, or just choosing to remember how powerful we really are.

Taking Steps

The ritual I am sharing with you today is informally referred to amongst my loved ones as "Doing the Spices." My parents are from Guyana, South America. Our ancestral roots are from West Africa, so I knew this ritual was ancestral but didn't know exactly where it was from. Then, I attended my first Yoruba wedding, and they did the same ritual. I have since learned that they also do versions of this ritual throughout the Middle East. We are truly all connected.

I "did the spices" as a blessing ritual at my cousin's wedding to celebrate her nuptials. My dad has done it at our family celebrations, and I have seen it performed at baptisms, weddings, birthdays, graduations and other celebrations. I have shared this ritual at a Goddess Circle of queens ready for a life reset.

Today, you will do this ritual as a Goddess Self-Love Blessing. Feel free to repeat it whenever you need a reset or restart in your life. I did this ceremony when I started my last book, *African Goddess Initiation*. This is a derivation of the traditional ceremonies.

Here's what you need:

1 Honey

2 Salt

3 Pepper or Hot Sauce

4 Vinegar or Lemon

Do What Works

Prepare your ritual space in the way that works best for you. You can do this ritual alone or with friends, at home or at a grand celebration. You may set up an ancestral or goddess altar.

Light white candles or the color that vibrates with the energetic frequency you wish to magnify. You may have crystals or soil to represent the earth element. Air can be represented with feathers or an instrument like a bell or drum. Pour water to refresh and salute your ancestors.

Each element represents a blessing. Feel free to substitute as needed. Some cultures use up to seven spices.

You may choose to start with a libation, and ask your ancestors to guide and protect you, thanking them for their wisdom and protection thus far.

Whether a baby blessing or wedding, we traditionally taste each element. You can bless yourself or have someone else bless you.

Here's what to say as you taste each element:

I now taste honey, nectar of Yoruba Goddess of Love and Beauty Oshun, for a sweet life. Thank you, life, for the sweetness.

I now taste pepper, the spice of Egyptian Goddess of War and Heat, Sekhmet, for a life where I know my power. Thank you, life, for the hotness.

I now taste vinegar to represent Iset, also known as Isis, Nubian Goddess of Faith and Magic, for a life where I learn from and easily transmute the bitter experiences. Thank you, life, for the bitterness.

I now taste salt, the gift of Igbo Earth Goddess, Ala, to symbolize preservation and a long, happy life. Thank you, life, for the earth.

Mantra: I celebrate the spice of life.

In the name of Yoruba goddess Oshun, Egyptian goddess Iset, the Zulu Rain Queen Modjadji, seductress Sitira of Guyana and Igbo goddess Ala, you are worthy and deserving of limitless joy. Claim your power now — and celebrate.

ABOUT ABIOLA

Empowerment coach, spiritual teacher and advice columnist Abiola Abrams is the founder of award-winning self-worth site Womanifesting.com. She is also the author of the award-winning advice guide, The Sacred Bombshell Handbook of Self-Love. Her latest book is coming out this summer: African Goddess Initiation-Sacred Rituals For Self-Love, Prosperity, and Joy.
Instagram *@abiolatv*

Orgasmic Manifestation

WITH ANITA KOPACZ

What you need:

2 cups of sea salt

3 drops of lavender essential oil

1 pyramid cut amethyst

A journal and pen

A candle

A jar of molasses

Sage

YEMAYA IS THE YORUBA GODDESS OF THE SEA. She is often depicted as a Black Mer Mother. Yemaya is said to be the mother of us all and is very compassionate and generous with her daughters. The Orgasmic Manifestation Ritual will bring you into the energy of infinite possibilities.

IF YOU DO DECIDE TO WORK WITH THE ENERGY OF YEMAYA, YOU SHOULD ALWAYS GIVE BACK TO THIS GODDESS.

I will explain how:

1 Draw yourself a bath with the sea salt and lavender. Light a candle, and be sure to cleanse the energy in the bathroom with sage before you step in the water. You can play music in the background to set the tone. You will essentially be making love to yourself in these sacred waters. Once you enter the bath, hold the amethyst in your hands. Think about what you want to manifest. Be as specific as possible. You can add this at the end of your intention: "This or something better for the highest good of all concerned."

2 Imagine that intention infused into the crystal. Place the crystal pyramid in the water in front of you and slowly begin to touch yourself. Use feather light touches all over your body. Circling your nipples and tantalizing your lower belly. When you feel your own waters flow, enter yourself with your two fingers, the pointer and middle. Listen to your body and what she wants. As you are ready to climax, call out your intention to the sky and imagine the top of the amethyst crystal pyramid sending your intention into the ethers as a beam from its tip. Take your two figures and place your sacred sexual waters on the crystal. Close your eyes and bask in this magical energy.

3 Write your intention and any other insights that you may have had during your experience in your journal.

How to thank Yemaya

IF YOU LIVE BY THE OCEAN, BRING THE JAR OF MOLASSES TO THE WATER. As you approach her sacred sea, feel the gratitude of your manifestations and the love for Yemaya. Pour the molasses in the ocean and say, "Thank you, Yemaya." You can add whatever you want to the prayer of gratitude.

ABOUT ANITA

Anita Kopacz is the author of the Simon & Schuster fiction novel, Shallow Waters. It is the second title that Charlemagne tha God will release on his imprint, Black Privilege Publishing on August 3, 2021. Anita is the former Editor-in-Chief of Heart & Soul Magazine and Managing Editor of BeautyCents Magazine. She is an award winning writer, a Spiritual Psychologist and a certified Tantra coach with a passion to see people thrive. Anita created the Zero F's Given campaign to raise awareness and help victimized and disenfranchised populations heal from sexual trauma, find their voice, and reclaim their power. She has helped thousands of victims through her work with Zero F's Given and being on the board for the Center for Safety and Change.

Through leading retreats around the world, working with private clients and storytelling, Anita fulfills her intention to awaken the divine simplicity, pleasure and joy in her life and others.

Instagram @anitakopacz

Loving The Luxurious Skin You're In

WITH BERNADETTE PLEASANT

Self-Care Practice

One of my favorite self-care practices is making a luxurious ritual out of loving the skin I'm in. I invite you to do the same. I love touch, but not just any touch. I enjoy the kind of touch that lands on skin with intention. Like poetry written on the body, I love touch that speaks without words.

The Ritual of Touch

To begin a ritual of touch, I invite you to select a personal elixir—a luscious oil, delicious lotion or creamy butter that smells and feels intoxicating as it glides across your skin. For me, it's all about the deep, natural luxury of coconut oil. I love to warm it up for the kind of massage that one can only give oneself—because we know exactly what feels good to our own bodies.

Self-love, for me, engages all the senses. So, I suggest setting the mood with intention. Lower the lights and light your favorite candles if that pleases you. Surround the space with your favorite music. I, personally, love Luther Vandross playing in the background when I'm setting my mood.

While the music is playing, allow the sound to float across your mind as the touch of your hands float across your body.

This is your time. Let yourself explore. Give your hands permission to ease into unexpected places. Maybe the back of your
hand wants to caress your forearm, glide across your breasts, massage your belly. Perhaps your inner arm finds itself wanting to brush against your outer thigh. There are so many pleasurable possibilities. Get curious about unfamiliar places, like noticing the sensation between your fingers as they glide across each part of your body. Whatever feels good to you, is just right.

It might be your desire to experience this massage before or after a long, slow bath. It's all good. This is intimate time with you. Rest and relax. Have a glass of your favorite beverage nearby so that you can sip it and enjoy luxuriating inside and out. Your body is a temple. Take your time.

Allow yourself to open and close your eyes as you please. You may feel more sensation when your eyes are closed, or you might experience the moment more fully when your eyes are open. Let yourself have the pleasure of playing with both.

LET YOUR BODY DISCOVER ITS OWN RHYTHM

Allow both hands, arms, and legs to be caressed. Thread your fingers gently between each toe. Offer soft and loving gratitude as your ankles slide up one leg and down the other. Lavish in the feel of your elixir against your skin. It might even get a little messy. So what? Indulge! You are worth every ounce of this experience.

I invite you to take a deep inhale of your candle's aroma. Look softly around the room. Maybe you'll catch a glimpse of your own shadow in the candlelight. Go ahead and dance slowly with it. Let yourself be moved by the mood of your music. For me, it's the sound of Luther singing, "A house is not a home" that reminds me that the body that encapsulates my essence is my "home".

This is our time to come home to our bodies, to love our skin, every luxurious hue that it's in. Be fascinated by every glorious hill and delicious valley. Be curious and explore your body like you've never done before. Allow the sounds and sensations that fill your space to seduce you into a love affair with your beautiful skin - every bit of it.

ABOUT BERNADETTE

Spirited and energetic, Bernadette Pleasant is a fiery and sensual speaker, somatic healer, Founder of The Emotional Institute and Creator of Femme!, a mind-body wellness program and 400 Years, a somatic-based anti-racism program. She is known for channeling her personal journeys and radical empathy into transformative, immersive experiences that support and celebrate people of all genders, colors, ages and sizes. She has transformed the lives of thousands of people around the world, inspiring them to become more self-expressed and empowered as their own badass selves.

Instagram: @bernadette_pleasant; www.theemotionalinstitute.com

Self Love Ritual

WITH CHEF AMEERA

Goddess Cacao

Serves 2:

8-10 oz filtered hot water

2 heaping tablespoons cacao

1 tsp pure vanilla

1 1/2 tablespoons mesquite

1 tablespoon maca

1 tablespoon ashwagandha

3 tablespoons coconut milk

2 tablespoons maple syrup

1 teaspoon rose water

Instructions:

1. Add all ingredients to a blender. Blend on high for 1 minute or until frothy.

2. Mix in Rose hydrosol and pour into your favorite mug. Sip and enjoy the magic of this ancient ceremonial drink.

Recipe Rituals

Eating high vibrational foods charged up with your intentions is a sacred act of self-love. Use this recipe to connect to your inner child and let her know she is safe, loved and is always welcome to come out and play.

As you gather your ingredients and prepare to make this decadent treat, allow the frequency of joy to permeate your thoughts. Think back to those things that made you joyful as a child. Use the recipe as a guide and allow your creativity and curiosity to flow. Add an extra pinch of love or a dash of cardamom. Allow the ingredients to speak to you and guide you.

Once you pour your cacao into your favorite mug, place your left hand over your heart and speak loving words of affirmation to charge it up. Enjoy!

ABOUT AMEERA

I began my love affair with food at the age of 8. I just LOVED to cook any and everything- especially Asian foods. And looking back to the young girl making egg rolls for my friends and family, I realize that it wasn't about the mechanics of cooking for me. The allure was in the way that my cooking made people FEEL. Now, instead of hoping that the people I cook for can feel the love, I KNOW they can! In 2012, I had a spiritual awakening that lured me to deepen my relationship with and understanding of holistic herb medicine and its connection to food. My rite of passage as a healer was fully recognized once I was able to see that my food not only tasted wonderful, it changed lives! As a Sacred Woman, under the nurturing guidance of Queen Mother Queen Afua, I evolved into the Food Alchemist I am today. I've cooked for celebrities and a myriad of clientele, including Demi Lovato, Sean "Diddy" Combs, Rihanna, and Common.

Instagram @chefameera

Self-Pleasure Ritual

WITH DEVI MAISHA

ONE OF MY FAVORITE SELF-CARE RITUALS IS A BATH FOLLOWED BY A SLOW SELF-PLEASURE (MASTURBATION) SESSION.

I START WITH A WARM BATH. Sometimes I add bubbles or essential oils, and sometimes I add flowers or orange slices. Anything that makes me feel luxurious and feminine. I like to bring in my bath tray and put a plate of snacks on it. I'll add fruit and maybe cheese and crackers. And of course, a glass of sparkling water or white wine. I turn off the bathroom light and light the candles, and the mood is set with a delicious playlist.

I SOAK IN THE BATH FOR 30 MINUTES TO AN HOUR – JUST ALLOWING MYSELF TO TAKE IN THE SCENTS AND THE SOOTHING FEEL OF THE WATER. I take time to touch my skin slowly and appreciate my body. I say "thank you, body, for housing my soul" over and over as I pay homage to my arms, legs, breasts, thighs…..all of my body. I slowly eat my food and drink my beverage, savoring the flavor of it all. I smile and invite the food and drink into my body as I sit back in the tub completely relaxed.

ONCE MY BATH IS DONE, I DRY OFF SLOWLY. Sometimes I lay on my bed and air dry. I rub my body down slowly with my body butter, taking time again to thank my body. It becomes a very sensual experience as I glide my hands over my thighs and stomach, over my breasts and hips. I look at each body part as I rub the body butter into my skin. Rubbing my own skin is arousing.

FEELING MY OWN TOUCH REMINDS ME OF MY BEAUTY AND SENSUALITY.

AFTER MY BODY HAS BEEN THOROUGHLY HYDRATED AND AROUSED, I BEGIN MY SLOW SELF-PLEASURE SESSION. Sometimes I light candles and put on music, sometimes I enjoy the silence. I spend anywhere from 20 – 60 minutes with my body. I give myself space to feel all the sensations without rushing the process. After climax, I put on something that makes my skin feel loved. That could be a cotton t-shirt or silk pajamas.

I USUALLY DO THIS RITUAL ONCE OR TWICE A MONTH. The whole process can take 1-2 hours. It's a beautiful way to honor myself.

ABOUT DEVI

Maisha is a Sacred Sexuality and Embodiment Guide who assists women with disrupting thought patterns that keep them from expressing their authentic, powerful, sensual selves. She can be found on Instagram and Facebook under Sensual Energy Alchemy and on Clubhouse under Devi Maisha.

Instagram: @sensualenergyalchemy; Facebook: SEAlchemy

Crystals into Self-Love

WITH DINAN RA

Self-Love Journey

In the journey back to loving ourselves, we will find that allies come in many different forms. The loving friend. The supportive coach or therapist. The perfect music to fit the mood. The right fragrance of essential oil that touches you in all the right places. Or maybe it's the perfect stone or crystal.

    In this self-love ritual, let us use the power of crystals to help us align with the love that is present for us at any time. Pink stones are most associated with love and can be found at any local crystal shop or online. My favorites for this work are rose quartz and kunzite. Master teacher of love and loving ourselves unconditionally. For this ritual, you will need only a small piece that can be carried around with you in your pocket or my personal favorite place - the BRA!!

Crystal Ritual

First, you'll want to cleanse this crystal and give it a job. Although, it is a stone that already knows what it is doing, it has a consciousness that can be communicated with and engaged. To cleanse your crystal ally, you can immerse it in the smoke of sage or Palo Santo or simply hold it in your hand with the intention to clear it of any past energies or programs. Remember, you are POWERFUL .

Next, tell your crystal friend what you would like it to help you with. This could be as simple as "Dear Crystal Ally, in the name of unconditional love, I charge you and ask that you help me love myself more. Thank you."

Keep your new ally with you as much as possible and watch how your perspective gently shifts over time to choose love more and more. Over and over again. Use your journal to take note of when you recognize this happening as you build a daily practice of writing about one thing that you love about yourself. I believe in you! You can do this.

ABOUT DINAN

I am a shapeshifter. A lover of life. A mother, a daughter, a friend, a giver, a lover, a receiver - I am all and all is me. I am an initiated shaman, a gifted sound healer, and a counselor who uses all the tools of my being to create opportunities for healing. I may sit and have a deep conversation with you. I may sing over you with my drum or singing bowl. I may lay minerals upon you. I may lay hands upon your energy centers. I may speak light language over you. Or I may co-create with the Universe something special just for you. It all depends on the needs of the individual I am working with. I offer services to meet different needs and I consider it a privilege to assist my fellow brothers and sisters.

I work with both corporate and individual clients, and am a brilliant public and motivational speaker and discussion facilitator.

Instagram @Dinan_ra

Self-Love Ritualsss!

WITH JAMEELAH ASSATA AUSET

SELF-LOVE IS SUCH A BEAUTIFUL REITERATION OF THE DIVINE'S LOVE FOR US. We show how much we appreciate the gift that we are by honoring and showing love to self. In the next two paragraphs I'm going to guide you through my favorite self-love rituals to boost me if I'm feeling off.

You'll need:

Paper
White candle
Stick of incense
Palo santo or sage
Lighter
Glass of water (fancy glass please)
Mirror
A list of synonyms for your favorite positive word (beautiful, cherished)
A nice big green yummy plant (optional)

Greetings, Goddess! So excited that you're getting this yummy self love ritual through my awesome sister, Goddess on the Go! I hope you enjoy it. All of my rituals are super short and sweet, but very powerful and immediately effective.

1 Okay, so if my energy is running low, the first thing that I do is identify the exact root of the problem. I get really clear on exactly what is ailing me by asking myself the source of the problem repeatedly. So for example, if I notice my energy is off and even if I believe that I am angry because my car window was just busted, I'll start asking "what's wrong?" Of course, the first answer is "my car window is busted, duh!" Then, I'll ask again, "What's wrong?" The next answer may be different: "I knew something was going to happen last night ,and I should've parked somewhere else." I'll ask again, "Goddess, what's wrong?" until I arrive at the root of the true problem:"I didn't trust my voice and speak up." I'm angry because ultimately I believe I should have listened to myself.

When you're doing this deep dive, keep probing until you run out of answers!

YOU'LL KNOW YOU'VE ARRIVED AT THE RIGHT ANSWER WHEN YOU SEE THAT THE EXTERNAL PROBLEM IS REALLY SOMETHING WITH INTERNAL ROOTS.

2 Make sure you have a space dedicated to you in the moment and time and quiet to do your ritual. What you're going to do here is lay out all of your materials and start your cleansing.

You set your intention while cleansing by thinking or even saying, "I'm here to boost my self love and cleanse/release self criticism/any energy that does not serve me."

You then cleanse by lighting your sage or palo and making your area smell and feel beautiful.

3 On the paper you write "I AM" in large letters. Place it in front of you where you can see it. Your mirror should also be placed in front of you where you can see your beautiful face.

You light your white candle and your incense stick. Sit and relax for a moment, taking it all in.

Then, from there, you start with "I am" and you go on a rampage, inserting every single positive word that comes to your mind.

Ex. I am capable, I am valuable, I am worthy, I am loved, etc."

(This is where you can use the list of synonyms that you wrote down.)

With this step, you repeat until you either run out of adjectives or until you are feeling the positive energy from the affirmations you just used.

Remember, it is important to repeat this portion of the ritual until you feel that new energy come in.

4 When you're ready to close out the ritual, you drink the water and repeat, "And so it is".

This ritual can be used at any time and any place whenever you need to remember who you are. I hope you enjoy! Feel free to let me know how this worked for you and if it's your favorite on instagram!

ABOUT JAMEELAH

Jameelah Assata Auset is a sage, professor, advocate, leader and the embodied prototype of the divine feminine. Known as the Growth Goddess and the Goddess Queen, Jameelah has been a catalyst for hundreds of women and girls in the categories of self love, healing, spiritual wisdom, confidence and growth for over 10 years. You can find her exploring the lands of the motherland as she settles into her home in Africa, spending lots of time with the loves of her life or working adamantly on her PhD. The Goddess Queen enjoys sincere thank yous, expanding her enterprise, writing, plant medicine ceremonies and luxury living.

Instagram @thegrowthgoddess

Hello Ritual

WITH KARLA LIGHTFOOT

ONE OF THE SIMPLEST AND MOST PLEASURABLE THINGS YOU CAN DO WHEN YOU WAKE UP IN THE MORNING IS TO SAY HELLO AND THANK YOU. Hello body, hello earth, hello home, plants, molecules, energy, Universe… and anyone, anything and everything else you'd like to thank. Hello, hello, hello every body and every thing!

THANK YOU, BODY, FOR BEING HERE WITH ME AND FOR ME.

Dancing this dance with me. Thank you, , for holding, nourishing, nurturing, birthing me, and allowing me and all the other beings to walk and live here on you. Thank you, home, for gifting me a place to cuddle and sleep. Thank you, plants, for providing clean oxygen for me to breathe. Thank you, Spring, Summer, Fall and Winter for showing me the ease of change and the seasons. Thank you, molecules, for coming together to create the vibration of life. Thank you, friends and playmates and other beings. Thank you again, Universe…Multiverse.

And after saying hello and thank you, would you be willing to hold, touch and caress your body? Or commune with the earth beyond speaking and feeling? What if you sensed the presence of body and earth as one and asked its energy to flow through you? Would you be willing to allow the energy of everything—the ocean, stars, trees, flowers, sun, moon and more to move through you? Can you allow yourself and your body to receive the vibration? Can you sense the potency of it all? Of you? What if your body is happy and grateful to be here for you? What if the earth, the Universe, and every single molecule are too? And what if they wish to communicate that in every moment? What if the energy of life is whispering, "Hello, little giant, I'm so grateful that you are here. You are so much bigger than you think you are. You are bright and beautiful. You shine as bright as the sun. You are Infinite. You are us and we are you. You have the capacity to transform anything and everything. You are magic. Have fun. Joy is your birthright."

And what about that which cannot be heard? Would you be willing to listen with your whole being? To own, acknowledge and embrace the truth about you? To receive the gratitude for you beyond the words and the silence. For your breath, your voice, your kindness and caring, your joy and laughter and all of your mistakes.

What if self-love is being willing to acknowledge all of life? What if it's being grateful for all of life? What if there's no right or wrong or good or bad? What if self-love is about communing and communicating with all of life? And All of Life includes You. Would you be willing to receive all of you and all of life?

WHEREVER YOU EXCLUDE YOU, THERE IS NO LOVE.

Every morning when you wake up, what if you would play and explore with this quick exercise? Acknowledge all of you as the contribution you are to all of life? And that all of life is to you... Let life flow, and vibrate and dance with you and for you. All of it. And all of you. Never ending. Ever-flowing. Life. Love. Energy.

I wonder what joy and possibilities that could create for you, for us and the World?

WAKE UP. HELLOOOO?!? AND THANK YOU, LOL.

ABOUT KARLA

Karla Lightfoot uses mind-body science, somatic and energetic exploration as well as sensual movement to create happier beings and bodies in the world. She is a Life adventurer and curious soul who is in awe of Mother Earth, the body and this magnificent Universe. Karla is a certified clinical medical hypnotherapist, a TRE® , and Access Consciousness® Certified Facilitator and a sensual movement instructor. Karla invites the life force energy that moves through everything and everyone into your world to co-create and move you into a future beyond your wildest dreams!

Instagram: @karla.lightfoot

Ritual of Everyday Feng Shui

WITH KATE MACKINNON

BY TRANSFORMING OUR HOME INTO AN OASIS OF BEAUTY AND PEACE, WE CREATE A space that invites love, prosperity, and health into our life, and a deep sense of inner well-being for ourselves and all who enter. And it feels so self-loving.

An easy way to create an oasis is also through our senses, wherever we may be. The following steps are simple things you can do for your inner space. You can do one or more of the steps, but doing them all together feels beyond self-loving.

In a favorite space where you like to meditate or just sit quietly, surround yourself with the following:

— An aromatic scent. Smell is our oldest sense and it is very important in loving ourself. You can use a scented candle, or spray or diffuse essential oil.
— Beautiful music or sounds, something soothing and calming that makes your spirit soar.
— Fresh flowers, an arrangement of your favorite mix of colors, that delight your eyes.
— A cup of your favorite hot or cold beverage, something that delights your tastebuds and warms your soul.
— Something to sit or lie on that feels good and is comfortable.

As you you sit or lie quietly, close your eyes, and in your mind's eye, go to a beautiful place, real or imagined that you like to go to — someplace you feel totally safe and free. Take a few deep breaths in and out, and experience it through ALL your senses.

— In this space, create an intention for something in your life that you desire and want to attract into your life, like love, prosperity or health. Be with it and experience it through all your senses.
— Say a mantra of your choice 9 times, then open your eyes and come back.

By going to this space, we are are consciously creating an oasis of positive life force energy both inside and outside. If you want, take out a notebook and write down where the space is and words that you would use to describe it. The place and the words you use describe what you want to bring into your home. They are the feeling of Feng Shui—creating harmony, flow and balance of positive energy in your space.

ABOUT KATE

Kate MacKinnon, a Certified Feng Shui Practitioner, has successfully consulted for businesses and individuals for over 20 years, bringing the power of Feng Shui to homes, offices, buildings, and land all over the country and, most recently globally. Prior to starting her business, Everyday Feng Shui, Kate had her own management technology consulting company and was Vice President of JP Morgan Chase. Kate's mission is to use Feng Shui and her experience to inspire all women to step into their power and greatness and live a life of beauty, grace, dignity and impact, at any age. You can find her inspiring talk on Women, Aging, and Visibility on TED.com.

Instagram @fengshuikate

Self-Love...Deep Breath

WITH KATHLEEN BOOKER

What is Self-Love?

It is remembering that, as A Course in Miracles says, 'Love created me like itself.'

The Breath gives you the strength, clarity and courage to rest in your truth.

THE TRUTH THAT LOVE CREATED YOU LIKE ITSELF

Take a moment and breathe that in.

YOU are Love.

YOU are Loved.

YOU are Loveable.

YOU are Love.

ABOUT KATHLEEN

Kathleen Booker is an effervescent native New Yorker. Her energy is infectious. Kathleen is passionate about Conscious Connected Breathwork therapy and knows first-hand the energy, healing, peace, and joy it creates in one's life. As a certified and insured Breathwork Coach, she has worked with many masters in the field of Conscious Connected Breathwork therapy. For over 10+ years, Kathleen has used her breath coaching and intuitive skills to support individuals in clearly identifying areas in need of growth, healing and focused goal creation. Kathleen's instinctive sense of what will motivate and empower her clients is the impetus for their transformation.

Instagram: @iamkathleenbooker

Self-Love Journal

WITH KIMBERLY SIMMS

Self-Love Tip

In 2014, my mother died of cancer. We had no idea she was terminally ill with lymphoma. 10 days after my family received the diagnosis she was gone. The day I left the hospital, I shut down and needed a life saving reset that I didn't know how I was going to find, but over time, I did. Although my mother was far from perfect, she was still my mom, and I missed her mothering, phone calls, advice, and protection. It was months of grief when one day something deep inside of me broke, and I surrendered to my deep sadness. In my grief, face full of tears and snot, I looked at myself in the mirror and, not recognizing who I was at that moment, I asked, "Who are you?" Then, I screamed, "WHO ARE YOU!" I couldn't answer, I didn't know in that moment who I was, but I knew who I wasn't…and I wasn't my exterior. I wasn't my jewelry, clothes, shoes, or makeup. I took it all off and stood there naked in the mirror. I finally felt seen and heard and whole again. I felt like myself without the grief, and I saw a deeper expression of myself naked and invulnerable…That day changed everything!!

Self-Love Practice

I wake up daily, get out of my bed and start my day naked in front of a full length mirror. I ask myself three times, "Who are you?" I respond with an affirmation I am holding in my heart for the day, for instance, "I am enough, I am worthy, or I am the LOVE I desire." I repeat the response three times, then I walk mindfully to my yoga mat to meditate. I set my timer for 5 minutes. During that time I focus on every inhale and exhale. I inhale for 5 breaths, hold for the count of five, and then exhale for the count of five until my timer goes off. This is tremendously great for my nervous system and decreases anxiety. On my altar, I keep honey or fresh fruits I can commune with in a total sensory meditation. Naked on my mat with honey or a piece of fruit, I activate all five senses by focusing on how it tastes, feels in my mouth, the sight and smell, also the texture and sound of what I am eating. I become completely aware in all my senses as I enjoy the food. I turn on music, and I move my body on my mat. I either do a set sequence like Sun Salutations or move my body freely to the music or both if my energy moves me. As I move my body, I contemplate deeply my desires for the day.

I VISUALIZE THE DAY EXACTLY HOW I DESIRE IT TO BE…AND I FEEL INTO IT AS I MOVE MY BODY.

I surrender to my emotions if anything comes up as I keep moving and desiring my favorite music. Afterwards, I self pleasure, which can bring me an orgasm or perhaps physical pleasure on my skin and muscles by way of touch and self massage. I like to use my orgasmic energy with intention and love that I activate in this way. I end my practice by setting my timer on my phone again for 5 minutes and writing in my journal. I write my gratitudes for life, my day, my children, whatever comes to mind and heart that reflects my present moment, unique and different each day. Then I close my journal and say out loud, "Amen, Asé, Aho and so it is-it is DONE." Amen means "yes". It is a Spiritual Affirmation to all I desire. Asé is a word used in different tribes and traditions in Africa, and it is an expression of reverence to my ancestors. It's a phrase that sets the affirmation and energy in motion...it activates the words. And Aho is a word used by indigenous people that means "Thank you to all in all." That's how I start most days... spiritually ready for the physical world!!

Self-Love Integration

I truly believe self-love is the best love. The way you love yourself gives you an opportunity to learn — by loving yourself first — how to love others the same way. For instance, giving ourselves patience, time, and consideration and becoming used to those dynamics will inspire expectation of the same behavior from our friends, family and loved ones. Learning how to radically approve of ourselves is an indication of unconditional love. If we don't require care, peace, kindness, and gentleness from ourselves, it feels unnatural and forced to ask it of others. We project our stories of the reasons we are not loving ourselves onto others and then believe these stories even when we are around people who want to love us. Providing ourselves with loving practices and rituals helps us to see love when it is being given without doubting it. We know love exists for us and from us. Our confidence when practicing loving ourselves grows, and then we can confidently love someone...anyone.

IT ALL BEGINS WITH THE RELATIONSHIP WE HAVE WITH OURSELVES FIRST.

I love myself from a place of peace, joy, and pleasure. The actions behind what I do for myself are fun and exciting, sometimes adventurous. Therefore, I have created a daily practice to make sure I am growing in love with myself more and more each day. I hope they pour love into you also..

ABOUT KIMBERLY

Kimberly Simms is a Mother of 4 children; Published Author; Inspirational Speaker; Fitness/Body Approval Model; Transformational Energy Worker and Coach; Femme! Attuned; Pleasure Revolutionary; Vinyasa 200hrsERYT Yoga Alliance Certified; Bikram Certified Yoga Instructor; regular Ashtanga Practitioner for the last 2 years; and nudist. Kimberly first started doing Yoga in her living room with Rodney Yee DVDs in 2000 because that was the only way she could afford Yoga, as a new mom. In 2014 she went through a period of depression and deep grief, after the sudden transition of her mother. Naked mirror work was an intuitive practice Kim used to help her find her way back to herself.

Instagram @nakedyogagoddess

I Am Ritual

WITH KRYSTAL ATHENA HUBBARD

SELF-LOVE/SELF-CARE has been a buzz phrase for sometime now. At the beginning of this movement, self-love was all about doing something special for yourself—getting your nails done, getting a massage, buying your favorite dessert. We have since discovered that self love is about the internal work to heal old wounds and trauma.

Self-love is hard, but you can use tools to support you during the hard parts. After all, getting through the hard parts makes that special dessert even sweeter! I love affirmations! Affirmations ground us in the moment, they remind us of our importance to ourselves first, and then to the world.

My favorite affirmation is: I AM Love. I AM Magic. I AM Whole. "I AM" statements define who you are, what you are, and where you are. They create an amazing boundary, completely impenetrable to any form of fuckery or tomfoolery. Affirmations are said out loud so you can hear your words as they sink into your being, making them real. I invite you to say the above affirmation out loud or to create your own "I AM" statement. Say them daily. Enjoy the journey of truly learning who you are! It's quite adventurous. I AM.

ABOUT KRYSTAL

Krystal Athena Hubbard is the owner of Bridging WorldsBotanica, an online shop based in Detroit, Michigan. I AM a Rootworker, Card reader, Penny Diviner, Teacher, Artisan Soap Maker, and I believe in living magic daily.
Instagram: @bridging_worlds_botanica; www.bridgingworldsbotanica.com

What Does Your Self-Love Look Like Today?

WITH LAUREN HARKNESS

WHILE ONE WEEK IT MAY LOOK LIKE A SAGE-SCENTED MUSIC–filled meditation or an essential oil-infused bath, another it might be laying on your floor in sweatpants, emoting, crying, or dropping in and out of long naps. We're so often sold our self-care through Instagram and "top tips" illustrations and an endless line of products, but don't forget, my loves, your self-care is YOURS.

THE KEY IS TO LISTEN, LISTEN IN THE SILENCE AND THE STILLNESS, FOR THE WHISPER. WHAT'S YOUR BODY TELLING YOU TODAY?

And it doesn't always come in a pink, perfectly-packaged box, or look like a scene from the highlight reel. Healing is messy, it's dark then it's light then it's dark again, it's a primal ugly cry into a pillow followed by an exuberant dance release. It's whatever you want it to be, and your body is always, always giving you signals of exactly what it needs.

I find that the more tools I add to my belt, the better I'm able to hear the call from my sacred vessel and match my practices with my deepest needs. Bonus: I'm also able to better hear and intuit the needs of my loved ones.

ABOUT LAUREN

ACTE Lauren Harkness is the Co-Founder of The Tantra Institute. At the Tantra Institute, Lauren develops and leads workshops, coaches private clients, and facilitates trauma release. She is passionate about Mental, Emotional, and Spiritual well-being. She is here to be a stand for everyone ready to heal and further ignite their sexual self: healthy, conscious, sovereign, and free! She teaches large group classes internationally and is a public speaker.

Instagram @sensualalchemistress

Inner Teen Self-Love Ritual

WITH LAURENA BRITTAIN

Be Your Inner Teen

One of my favorite and most powerful Self-Love rituals involves reconnecting with our Inner Teen. This is the older, not as popular sibling of our beloved Inner Child. Most people love Inner Child work because what's hard about scooping up and adoring that tiny fragile aspect of yourself that needs care and attention? We can all look at a small two-year-old and see them as vulnerable and needing protection. It can be a whole other story with our Inner Teen. They're often angry and sullen, bitchy and downright rude. But the reality is that they desperately need our attention and validation just as much as that small inner child.

Shadow work addresses the parts of ourselves that we exiled because they weren't accepted by our friends or families and society. The process begins in childhood but ramps up significantly during puberty when being included by our friends becomes really important, like life or death important. We will literally disown entire aspects of Self just so that our friends will 'like' us. This is normal and completely natural. In shadow work, we welcome those parts back and re-integrate them so that they stop wreaking havoc on our lives and getting in the way of what we're trying to create.

One of the best ways to spot these exiled parts is to start witnessing where you are resisting change and the things you want. Your Authentic Self is trying to claim its divine right, and essentially your Inner Teen is having an absolute meltdown and tantrum. What follows is a ritual I created to walk my client through reclaiming exiled aspects of self. I always recommend working with a professional trained in holding space for painful memories when doing this kind of work to offer support should it become overwhelming. I cannot emphasize enough how important it is to have the right support system in place before you undertake any kind of deep healing work.

Perform the Ritual

Items you'll need for this exercise:

* A quiet place where you won't be disturbed.

* A playlist with a collection of your favorite songs from middle school and high school

* 2 large sheets of paper

* Coloured pencils, markers, or paints. Whatever products you like to be creative with.

* A journal for writing

* A candle

* Some dark chocolate

* A safe place to burn your paper (a fire pit, deep metal sink, or metal pot with a lid to contain ash).

1 Think about your favorite songs from when you were growing up. Create an Inner Teen playlist. It's best to do this over a week as you prime your subconscious to bring up feelings associated with that time. Be very gentle and remember that adolescence is usually a turbulent time and you may be caught off guard by how emotional and

unsettled you feel. Always good to have a supportive friend on stand-by to talk over what's coming up.

2 Over the week, be sure to jot down any memories that start swirling around in your thoughts. Pay close attention to your dreams as we often try to make sense of our experiences while we sleep. Make notes about any symbolism in them, like feeling suffocated, trying to talk and express yourself but no words coming out, walking into rooms and being invisible, etc.

3 Schedule your ritual in advance, make it a date with yourself and be sure to keep it — the absolute worst thing you can do is not show up for your Inner Teen. Visualize that your Authentic Self is about to sit down with your younger self and listen and validate everything they have to say, regardless of how ugly or unpalatable it is.

4 On the day of your meeting, listen to your playlist as you organize your space for the ritual. Think back to that young woman and what she would have liked, what drinks or treats, how the space should feel so that she's super comfortable and accepted. Think about the people who validated you when you were younger and the things they did that made you feel that way.

5 At the time of your meeting, sit down and make yourself comfortable. Turn off the music, light a candle, center, and ground and quietly focus your attention inward. Ask your Inner Teen if she feels safe enough and ready to share. Listen closely, if the answer is 'No,' DO NOT proceed. Thank her for being brave enough to even show up, tell her that's it ok, that she has a right to her boundaries and that you're willing to wait as long as necessary for her to feel safe. Sit with her for a while and reschedule for another time. Keep repeating this process until she trusts you enough to share what she's been carrying for years.

Once the answer is 'Yes,' take out your first large piece of paper and break it up into 3 sections. At the top of the first section write 'Family,' section 2 'Friends,' and section 3 'Society.' Ask your Inner Teen what messages she received from each of these areas as she reached puberty. More than likely the answers will bounce around from one section to another. You may need to ask her to clarify who she feels the message came from, and it may have come from multiple sources. For example, my Teen heard that it was super important to be THIN, KIND, SMART, and above all else, I internalized there was no room for screwing up, so I needed to be PERFECT and INDEPENDENT.

> FOR EXAMPLE, MY TEEN HEARD THAT IT WAS SUPER IMPORTANT TO BE THIN, KIND, SMART, AND ABOVE ALL ELSE, I INTERNALIZED THERE WAS NO ROOM FOR SCREWING UP, SO I NEEDED TO BE PERFECT AND INDEPENDENT.

This is not necessarily what you were explicitly told by the people around you, it's the message you heard.

6 Take some time to really let it sink in how these were simply messages from the outside world that you internalized as the "TRUTH" about who you needed to be in order to be loved and accepted, but in reality, they were only other people's opinions.

7 Now take a thick pen or pencil and scribble out the word and replace it with its opposite. So in my example, for THIN, you would

replace it with FAT, KIND with MEAN, PERFECT with IMPERFECT, and INDEPENDENT with DEPENDENT. These are more than likely the aspects of yourself that you have exiled to be accepted by the people orbiting around you. Growing up, I was not allowed to be fat, mean, imperfect, and dependent, and I would do everything in my power to hide or avoid these aspects of myself, to the point I eventually forgot they ever even existed. The issue is that these are natural aspects of being human and by disowning them you're neglecting and creating dissonance in your daily life. For example, now everything about food revolves around fat/thin instead of hungry/satiated, or the way I'm setting boundaries in my life is around appearing kind/mean versus what's healthy/unhealthy for me. Your disowned aspects of Self are the driving force behind your behaviors and the way you're showing up in the world versus what you truly want and supports your creative energy.

8 Take out your second sheet of paper. At the top of the sheet write "MY AUTHENTIC SELF IS PERFECTLY IMPERFECT, WHOLE & COMPLETE: I NOW RECLAIM AND WELCOME MY EXILED PARTS." For each of the items that you have listed, write "I reclaim _____". So in my case, I would write "I reclaim being dependent," "I reclaim being mean," etc, then you can branch out and think of all the other things that you were never allowed to be. They may be flooding in now and they were often things you were shamed for …. "I reclaim being angry and foul, aggressive, stupid, a loose woman, weak, needy, unable to say no, etc."

9 Take your first sheet of paper and say a prayer over it. Apologize to your Inner Teen that she received these messages and explain to her that they were not hers to own. Validate that being accepted while growing up was vitally important, so important that anyone would hide aspects of themselves to be loved. Explain that by burning this sheet you are now giving those messages back to where they came from and reclaiming all the exiled aspects of Self. Take your first sheet and burn it safely, visualizing all the internalized messages finding their way back to the people who gave them to you.

10 Sit for a moment quietly and journal any additional thoughts that come up for you. Thank your Inner Teen for being so brave and being honest and showing up for you. Bring your attention back to the present moment, reground yourself and center, have some of the chocolate and blow out your candle, closing out the process.

11 Find a safe place to post your second sheet of paper, somewhere that you'll see it every day as a reminder but that you don't run the risk of someone who might judge you when seeing it. Practice being all of the things you've reclaimed in a visualization. See yourself being mean as a natural reaction to being hurt, see yourself being angry as a natural reaction to injustice, see your dependency on other people as a natural reaction to being a social creature who depends on her tribe for support and meaning. Now understand that you have healthier options and tools for some of those behaviors now that you have agency to choose who you want to BE. For example, you can choose to set healthy boundaries with people who hurt you, you don't need to be mean, and you can use your anger to take action on injustices instead of channeling it into aggressive behaviors that don't necessarily serve you.

Over time and through the use of this practice, your behavior will become a natural expression of your Authentic Self, allowing yourself to realign with the full capacity of who you are, and will create the space for you to consciously choose the life you want to create and manifest.

ABOUT LAURENA

Laurena is a relationship and dating expert who is on a mission to disseminate quality, relatable, actionable information to support women in creating a life and choosing a life partner in divine alignment with their Authentic Self. She offers personal coaching, workshops, and retreats. You can check out her point of view here:

Instagram: @findlove.bsmitten; www.bsmitten.com

CPR Method

WITH LOTUS LALOBA

WHEN YOU INVITE THE FEMME DIVINE IN TO GUIDE YOU, YOU COME FROM A PLACE OF OVERFLOW IN EVERY AREA OF YOUR LIFE WITH EASE & EFFICIENCY.

The CPR Method gets you into alignment mentally & spiritually.

You ready for the ultimate blueprint that can be used daily to focus on YOU? In order for you to SHOW UP fully in any area of your life (relationships, work, finances, purpose) you have to have healthy, whole self-love. It's never too early to shift from hustle and grind to harmony & grace. Use these 3 shifts to jumpstart happiness in your day. That's how aligned Goddesses live their lives.

CPR stands for:

Create to Connect

Praise on Purpose

Recover to Resonate

Shift #1 Create to Connect:
Helps you tap into all the magic that's around you.

Creativity is the direct connect to a solid foundation with Source, God, The Universe (whoever you identify with). It shows you the first step to experiencing excitement for life by waking up and creating. We are able to bring life into the world in every way possible through our practice of creativity. When we take the time to tap into your inner artist, it brings about major alignment. There's something about finding your true self in an activity that moves you. It can unleash inspiration, inner peace knowing that you are brilliant and capable of more than you know. There are so many ways you can connect via creativity. Activities like making your bed, your favorite morning drink or coloring are a great start.

Shift #2 Praise on Purpose
An elevated way to experience & express gratitude.

We praise to recognize that life is a gift. It gives us the space to celebrate the good and the not so good, because they give us perspective on what we do want in our lives. Praise is the space where Joy really comes through and does her thang. We get to see the miracles in everyday life, like our humanity, nature, and making it through the mistakes we've made by choosing love instead. It's not hard to get into a praisin' vibe either! You start with saying "Thank you" as much as you can, making a daily gratitude list or a playlist of songs that make you happy to be here now.

Shift #3 Recover to Resonate:
Let your body show you how powerful you are.

Your body wants to help you release the low vibes to make space for the good and juicy ones. Using the full body (head to toe) to recover reminds the mind & body that they can work in harmony to handle anything.

    Cultivate time every single day to drop out of your head and into your body. This is so crucial to your overall well-being. When we starve ourselves of this sacred time to reconnect, we start to experience unwanted situations. Our bodies are in constant movement, but when we consciously move them, we receive the help we need to enjoy our lives. You can start by honoring your breath, dancing, yoga, a good workout, or even just mindfully walking can do wonders for you!

Now that you have the ultimate blueprint for a good start to your morning, the time out to pick 1 to 2 activities for each shift. Whip out your journal and write down how each activity makes you feel when you do it too. This helps you witness your patterns and develop healthier habits that will expand your mind in the best ways. Can't wait to see you shining brighter love.

ABOUT LOTUS

Lotus LaLoba is a mystic practitioner who holds space for WOC to eradicate generational trauma and create a new legacy of limitless Self Love. Her core spiritual modalities are Energy Healing & Beauty Magick.

Instagram @lotuslaloba

Crystals for Self-Love
WITH MERCEDES

Here is a 3 step process using crystals that will help you regain self-love.

1 Self-Forgiveness

Before you receive love, you must be willing to heal and give yourself love. Release what no longer is serving you or what may be getting in your way from fully opening up your heart to unconditional love. Using the energy of the Aquamarine crystal — Aquamarine is a great crystal to aid in self-forgiveness — begin to create a list of all the people and things you need to forgive yourself or them for. Take the crystal in your receptive hand, and add a Clear Quartz crystal in your dominant hand — Clear Quartz crystal amplifies your desires and intentions — and say out loud, "I forgive myself for…" as you go down your list. Once you are done, sit with the crystals. Thank them for helping you release and make sure to ground with a Smoky Quartz crystal, which will help soothe any emotions that may come up. It's okay to allow whatever emotions, thoughts, feelings that come up to come up and through — that is how you have breakthroughs. Allow yourself to feel, and remember to be gentle and compassionate with yourself — this is not an easy process; however, it is a rewarding one.

2 Self-Acceptance

Remembering who you truly are is key to accepting yourself and that you are a divine expression of source/God/Goddess. It is okay to make mistakes. You are not perfect — no one is! It is how you treat yourself and what you say to yourself that is important. Affirmations / Womxntras are keys to helping you receive more love. Take some time to write and say the following affirmations: "I am worthy", "I am divine love", "I deserve love", " I am loved" (you can add any additional affirmation that you wish that makes you feel loved). If you can, grab a hold of Rhodonite and/or Rhodochrosite crystal — Rhodonite helps us feel less vulnerable and more courageous in receiving love and Rhodochrosite helps release trauma and opens up your heart chakra. Place the crystals in your hands and repeat the affirmations over and over until you feel the energy of the crystals/words wash over you. It's okay if you don't feel anything, the work is still being done. I also like to write affirmations on post-it notes and stick them on the mirror so when I look at myself I am reminded to say them.

3 Self-Care

GIVE YOURSELF TIME TO BE AND DO WHAT YOU LOVE

Go for a nature walk, eat healthy meals, sing, dance, wear some fun/sexy clothes and your favorite lipstick or lipgloss, meditate, etc. Do something that uplifts your spirit and takes care of your vessel (body), because you are WORTH IT!!!

Here's a quick mediatation you can do with the Rose Quartz crystal.

Take your Rose Quartz crystalm — Rose Quartz helps you to find forgiveness, compassion and assist with unconditional love) and place it on your heart chakra (chest area) or you can hold it in your hands. Make sure to find a comfortable position and breathe deeply a few times until you feel relaxed and calm. As you continue to breathe repeat the following *"I am love, I am loved, I have love, love is me"* over and over again in your head, and as you keep saying it, imagine a pink light emanating from your crystal and going straight into your heart. This light is glowing and growing bigger until it surrounds you fully. It encompasses your entire being. You are now inside this pink bubble of love and light.

As you breathe, imagine this light filling you up with all the love from the universe, the earth, and with all the love and light you deserve by divine right. It is your birthright to receive love and joy. Take this in as you continue to breathe, knowing that you have access to this light and love always. Breathe and watch as the light goes back into your heart space, reminding you of how loved you are. Continue to breathe in and out and, when you are ready, open your eyes, wiggle your hands and toes, and thank the Rose Quartz crystal and yourself for the love you have received. Giving yourself time to be still and receive is the ultimate practice of self-love. Amen Ase Aho! Other great self-love crystals to use: Mangano Calcite, Ruby, Watermelon Tourmaline.

ABOUT MERCEDES

Mercedes is the creatrix of CalienteSoulExpressions™. She is a certified Crystal Reiki Healer, Reiki Master, Intuitive Consultant, Femme Attuned Teacher, Revelation Breathwork Facilitator, and Psychic Medium. Her knowledge of crystals and their healing properties combined with her ability to attune to energy fields help her to be of service to those in need.

Mercedes is also an artivist — she combines her love for the arts with her passion for justice on a platform that helps bring awareness to humankind. **Instagram, Facebook, Youtube: @CalienteSoulExpressions; www.calientecreatrix.com**

Astrostyle Summer Solstice Ritual

WITH OPHIRA & TALI EDUT: THE ASTROTWINS

ON JUNE 20, 2021, AT 11:32 AM EDT, the Sun will reach its highest point in the northern hemisphere sky. This marks the official summer solstice for those of use above the equator, a time to bring illumination to parts of our lives that are hidden, confusing or stuck.

While it's ideal to do this ritual at the time of the solstice, we also believe that the power of intention is everything. So if you're reading this within a day or so of the solstice, we recommend doing it anyway!

Below are the instructions and supply list for your solstice flower wheel and ritual.

Supplies for Your Ritual:

Flowers (8 minimum) or at least 10 petals from a single flower. Alternatively, you may also use leaves, herbs, or another "green" that has been soaking up the Sun all spring.

4 small crystals or stones

Votive or pillar candle (1 or more)

Notebook

Directions:

1 Find a flat surface for your Solstice Wheel. It can be the floor, a tabletop, a tray, etc.

2 Place your candle(s) in the center of this surface as a symbol of the illumination that the Sun rays bring

3 Using flowers, petals, leaves—or anything else that has bloomed in the Sun—make a ring around the candle(s). Leave a couple inches or more of space between the candles and the ring, as you'll be placing a couple things there.

4 The heat and energy of the Sun can be intense, so it's a good idea to add some earthy, grounding elements like crystals or stones. You can place them in between the flowers. Or, you might set them at the north, south, east and west points to represent the 4 directions.

The AstroTwins Summer Solstice Ritual:

1 **First, let's INVITE IN THE SUN.**
Light the candle in the middle of your Solstice Wheel. As you do, you can recite these words (or have someone who is participating in the ritual with you do so:

   "With this flame, I invite in the energy of life-giving light of the Sun. On this longest day of light, I ask the Sun to illuminate new possibilities for my life and for my loved ones. I ask the Sun to show me what is next along my path."

2 **Think about the brightest area of your life right now**
Sometimes, when we do rituals, we focus on what is missing or what we want to manifest. But it's just as important to put attention on the things that are already working and to bring gratitude there. Gratitude is fuel for the manifestation tanks. The more of it you can feel, the more magnetic you become.

So, what is that bright spot for you? Maybe it's something major, like "I just got engaged and I'm totally in love." Or maybe it's something small like, "I love my the vibe in my office right now" or "I'm feeling really good about my summer yoga practice." Or, "My kids are the light of my life."

Whatever it is, let's take a minute, close your eyes and revel in that bright feeling.

3 **Now, think an area of your life that could really use some of that bright illumination.**
This should be something that you want to deal with over the summer, something that you are so ready to change. Got it? Okay. This is going to be your summer solstice wish, and in a minute we are going to write that down. But first...

Close your eyes and visualize this situation or the area of life in need of illumination. While you don't have to figure out the "how," let's do a little imagining. If everything was working with this situation, what would your life be like? What would you be doing with your days? Who would be with you? What types of people would you be spending time with? What would you be wearing?

4 **Write this as a summer solstice wish.**

A few examples:

"I wish to create pleasure and romance in my relationship this summer."

"I wish to find the perfect apartment to live in for the next two years."

"I wish to be guided to the next phase of my career."

"I wish to be creatively unblocked so I can write the next chapter of my novel."

Write your wish onto a piece of paper. Fold it up and place it inside the Solstice Wheel.

---

5 **Take one of the flowers from your circle and remove a petal.** Read your wish aloud (or close your eyes and say it to yourself in your head), then blow the wish into the petal. Place the petal inside the ring of your Solstice Wheel, on top of your paper.

6 **After the solstice (within 48 hours), take the wish petal out into nature.**
Find a favorite spot, like an area in a park, your own yard (if you have one) or a shore you love walking along. Thank the Sun for energizing your wishes, then let the petals fly into the wind. As you release them, have faith that the universe carry them off and deliver your message to the right source!

YOUR SOLSTICE WISH ACTIVATION IS NOW IN THE BEST HANDS THE UNIVERSES HANDS. AND SO IT SHALL BE.

ABOUT THE ASTROTWINS

OPHIRA & TALI EDUT: Identical twin sisters Ophira and Tali Edut, known as the AstroTwins, are professional astrologers who reach millions worldwide. Through their website Astrostyle and as the official astrologers for ELLE magazine, they bring the stars down to earth with their lifestyle and coaching-based approach to horoscopes. They've created astrology sections for multiple media properties, including Refinery29, Parade, and Lifetime TV. Bestselling authors, they've written a collection of books, including AstroStyle, Love Zodiac and Momstrology (their #1 Amazon bestselling parenting guide) and their own brand imprint annual horoscope guides.

Instagram @astrotwins

Creating Space Ritual

WITH MONICA SHAH

MONEY IS AN ENERGY. An energy that needs to be worked with, celebrated and most importantly, paid attention to. The problem is that most of us are filled up with fear of not having enough, guilt about making the wrong money decisions, or shame in asking for money. With all this stuff rolling around, it's no wonder we can't seem to attract the abundance we deserve. It's time to let go!

Here's how to let go of that old money stuff and call in new wealth and prosperity.

FIRST, IMAGINE AN IMAGE OF LAKSHMI - the Hindu goddess of wealth. It doesn't matter if you don't know what she looks like - just picture a beautiful goddess. Lakshmi always has one palm open to receiving and one palm up in defense. She says yes to what is good for her and no to what is not working. Take that stance yourself, one palm open, saying yes, and one palm up, saying no. Think about what you want more of - what you are saying yes to. Think about what you want to stop or release - what you are saying no to. Close your eyes and breathe.

Now, make a list of all the things you want, the more specific the better. Next to each item, put a price — how much money will it cost? Look it up if necessary. Add pictures if you like. Hold this list to your heart and SEE yourself having those things.

Then, add up the prices on one or more of those items. Determine what you could sell or offer to generate that amount of money over the next 90 days.

Then, see yourself getting those new clients or selling those new offerings. Who will buy them? What do those people look like? How does it feel when they say yes? Draw pictures of your new clients or consumers.

Each morning, pick up your list of desires and your pictures of your consumers. Breathe them in and visualize them coming for 1-2 minutes.

THEN LET IT ALL GO (THIS PART IS IMPORTANT). AND GET TO WORK! KNOW THAT YOUR DESIRES AND YOUR CLIENTS ARE COMING!

ABOUT MONICA

Monica Shah is a seven-figure business coach with an MBA from the Kellogg School of Management. She shows entrepreneurs how to earn more and handle their money in simple, practical ways that lead to more freedom, meaning and impact. She believes every woman should have a bank account with her name on it – and know how to fill it with the money she needs to live the life that she wants.

Instagram: @Monicacshah

Yoni Steam Ritual

**WITH ALICIA HUDSON
THE HONEYDEW HOLISTICS**

YONI STEAMING IS A SACRED SELF-CARE PRACTICE that has been used by indigenous people for centuries to heal and tone the womb. This beautiful ritual helps nourish the vagina and allows us to tap into our divine feminie energy.

Steaming helps to release stagnant energy, emotions, and blockages. It also helps to eliminate toxins and waste in the womb. Doing yoni steams improves circulation, which enhances the body's own healing mechanisms. On an emotional level, steaming activates a connection to the sacral chakra and is a powerful act of self-love.

The Ritual

1 Start by turning on some music to vibe to, smudge your body from top to bottom and your space, and light some candles.

2 Next, bring 2 quarts of filtered water to boil. Add 1 cup of the Honeydew Holisitcs Wise Womb Steam. Simmer on the stove for 5 minutes. This will bring out more of the essential oils in the herbs. Turn off heat and allow water to cool with the lid on for an additional 5 minutes.
You will need to let it cool off for a few moments before you can sit over it. Please be careful when you sit to not burn the sensitive tissues of your vulva.

3 Place the pot of herbs under your open seated chair, yoni stool, or simply squat over it. Make sure you wear socks and wrap a large blanket closely around you and the pot, so all the heat stays inside.

The steam should feel warm and gentle. If it feels too hot, stand up to avoid burns.

4 Stay sitting, wrapped in a warm blanket, over the steam for about 30 minutes. You can also gently massage your lower abdomen to further enhance the healing process.

5 After the steam is finished, move directly from the seat to bed, and wrap yourself up with warm covers. Lie down for at least one hour, or ideally for the entire night.

6 Steam every month before and/or after each menstrual cycle for optimal womb health.

    Do not steam if you are pregnant or think you may be pregnant!

    Do not steam if you are currently bleeding, have an active vaginal infection, open wounds or an IUD.

ABOUT ALICIA

I created my business Honeydew Holistics in 2018 to assist other women in becoming plant-based, learning how to heal their wombs by using their food & sacred herbs as medicine, and to prepare for & maintain a healthy pregnancy. I offer support through every stage.

On April 17, 2021, I opened my Honeydew Holistics Womb Wellness Shop in Downtown Brooklyn. I offer yoni steaming, holistic doula services, and have an apothecary section where I make custom herbal teas and steams.

Instagram @honeydewholistics

Circle of Power

WITH SHANNON CARSON

THIS IS AN NLP (NEURO LINGUISTIC PROGRAMMING) TECHNIQUE I use for a variety of things. You can use it before an interview, performance, speech or any event where you need to feel at your very best and in confident, tip top form. Or you can use it as a Circle of Protection for when you need to feel that you are safe and have a shield of protection around you.

I recommend having a favorite piece of music to play during this exercise to help you anchor this feeling. Something that you connect with that helps you to feel powerful and unstoppable.

Some suggestions are:

Diamonds by Rihanna

Theme from Rocky

Champion by Barns Courtney

Unstoppable by Sia

Something Inside So Strong by Union of Sound

It's about YOU feeling powerful, so use a song that works for you.

IN A STANDING POSITION, breathe deeply in and out 3 times, relaxing your body as much as possible with each breath. Imagine that on the floor in front of you is a gold circle. See it, hear it resonate, KNOW it is there. This is your Circle of Power or Circle of Protection.

When you are ready, step into the circle and see, hear, feel smell and taste what it is like to step into that power and protection. In this circle you are completely powerful and completely protected. Everything you need, all of your resources are in this circle. It feels GOOD to have this power, this protection around you and around all that you desire to create. There is no fear, no anxiety, no negativity in your thoughts, feelings or memories. Stand in your circle, and in this place of power and protection, speak to whatever you would like to speak to from this powerful place. Hear and feel your inner voice speaking confidently, wisely, filled with truth, power and protection. Now, play your piece of music, anchoring in this feeling of powerful, protected, unstoppable confidence.

You may wish to record this exercise for yourself.

Know you can recreate this circle anytime you need to create total confidence!

ABOUT SHANNON

Shannon Carson is an Intuitive Empathic Energy Healer for People, Pets and Spaces, Wellness Workshop Facilitator and Practitioner Trainer, NLP Practitioner, Reiki Master and Femme! Teacher

Instagram: @ShannonCarsonWellness;
www.ShannonCarsonWellness.com

Breathe into Body Love

WITH TANIA STERLY

WE AS WOMEN DRESS OUR BODIES EVERY DAY and sometimes we're in love with our bodies and sometimes we forget to be compassionate with our gorgeous temples. Even if you can't swoon over your body right now, you can absolutely accept where your body is at this moment.

Take a sacred pause and breathe into body love

Right now, sit back, your back could be leaning against up against a sofa or headboard, have your feet and legs relaxed and supported.
    Wear something soft and cozy, nothing restrictive, kick your shoes off, take a break, close your eyes and breathe. Place your right hand on your heart, place your left hand on your belly and now breathe in deep to the bottom of your belly, 123, breathe out, 321. Now I want you to imagine that part of your body that that you love.

Is it your smile?

Is it your butt?

Is it your legs?

Is it your shoulders?

What part of your body do you love showing off when you get dressed? Think of how sexy that area of your body is when you flaunt it flirt it, when you reveal it or conceal it. Now take that same love and appreciation for that area of your body that you love and appreciate and breathe into body love, breathe into that area of your body that you're not so happy with right now:

Is it that belly of yours that got a little bigger and softer?

Is it those thighs that keep getting curvier?

Is it your ankles?

Is it your crazy hair what's your hair doing right now?

Is it your cheeks?

Breathe into body love that same love and appreciation you have for those sexy hips, those beautiful lips. You're going to breathe into the areas that maybe you're not accepting right now. Now breathe in, 1 2 3, breathe out, 321, breathe in and out again and now breathe from head to toe and sprinkle a ray of pink glittery sparkling light through your body from head to toe and repeat your breathing to body love mantra, whatever that mantra is:

"I love my hips, my lips and my intelligence"

"I love my stretch marks on my tummy because I am so grateful I birthed a child"

"I love my legs even though my ankles are getting thicker"

"I love my legs because they're strong and healthy and allow me to dance"

So again, breathe into body love. This is the body that you adorn with dresses with jewelry, with style, with colors that make you flourish and express yourself. Take it easy on yourself, thank your body, love your body, and breathe into body love from head to toe .

DO THIS EXERCISE FIRST THING IN THE MORNING when you wake up or at night before you go to bed. Love and appreciate that beautiful body of yours and all of its changes. Embrace your beauty, embody your style, and continue to use style to express the beautiful, vibrant woman that you truly are!

ABOUT TANIA

Tania Sterl, CEO & Founder of Sterl on Style, is a Style Strategist, Fashion Expert, Speaker, and published writer. Tania combines her 18 years' experience as a fashion designer with an image consultant certification and her intuitive approach to style, curating a person's style in alignment with their current role, future goals, unique personality, profession and lifestyle. Styling industry leaders, authors, speakers, influencers, and thought leaders across all industries, for TV appearances, Tedx Talks, interviews, promotions, every day work dressing and more, Tania shows women the importance of investing in their image to elevate their image and influence, getting women dressed and ready to be seen as the experts and leaders they truly are.

Instagram: @sterlonstyle

Self-Value and Money

WITH RHONDA

WHEN WE BEGIN TO HAVE CONVERSATIONS ABOUT SELF-LOVE, our self-value and money are a great place to start. By inspecting our habits around money and what we think we deserve in life, we are able to see clearly as to if we have been practicing self-love or not.

Do you feel better when you spend money? Has retail therapy run you into large amounts of credit card debt? Do you buy things to fit in? The latest phone, bag, or shoes? Or spend money to feel good about yourself? This type of spending is subconscious and may have roots in childhood or past experiences.

The connection between self-worth and money is evident by our personal accomplishments, setting and hitting life goals, and yes, our bank account. We can also include how much debt we've acquired, our credit score, and yes, our bank account balance.

Let's also not confuse having money with having self-worth and self-love. The two definitely do not account for one another. I'm simply stating if you don't have peace of mind around your finances, then there is an energetic disconnect that should be addressed. Why? Because money is currency, energy coming in and energy going out. If your money isn't treating you right, then there is a good chance that you haven't been treating you right either... ouch!! Did I just say something?

Our relationship with money should be about your financial goals and feeling good about your choices. Making good financial decisions and reaping the rewards of having a life that you can enjoy, doing the things you want to do, when you want to do them.

Self-love is a long game, and most of it comes with experience and conscious effort to do the work towards self-mastery. We must actively unpack our thought process and be award of our main sticking points.

Journal this:

1. What is your earliest memory of money?

2. Do you believe you are worthy of a prosperous life?

3. What is your own definition of abundance?

4. How does your upbringing affect your views on money?

5. What is the biggest asset needed to be abundant?

6. "Money can't buy happiness." Is this true? Why or why not?

7. Which aspects of your life are defining your abundance?

8. Reflect on your recent financial decisions - what do they teach you about abundance?

9. What would your life be like if you could live in abundance for a year?

You can schedule a complimentary session with Rhonda at https//Calendly.com/wellnesspartner/financial-consultation.

ABOUT RHONDA

As a Health and Wellness Coach, Rhonda provides tools for Mind, Body, Heart and Soul Renewal. Rhonda services through workshops/seminars, speaking engagements, group and one-one-one consultations and coaching. Rhonda hosts workshops and seminars on the body's normal functions and methods of natural healing. Rhonda is also an Aroma Therapist who utilizes the power of scent for mental and emotional healing. Recently, due to need of financial health in most Americans that Rhonda has observed, Rhonda has added Financial Wellness to her Services, creating a 4-fold wellness collaboration. Rhonda Provides a Financial Needs Analysis, a type of Financial GPS which assists individuals with getting out of debt or paying off debts sooner, protecting their income, and properly saving for life after the working years.

www.Be4EverWell.com; Facebook: @be4everwell;
Twitter: @be4everwell; Instagram: @Be4everwell

Listening to our Intuitive Knowing is Self-Love

WITH VANESSA C. CODORNIU

WHEN WE LOOK AT OUR LIVES, we may notice that there are moments where we may have felt we went along with the program, didn't speak up or continued down avenues that were harmful to us in the long run. We may have had a feeling, a hunch, a sensation or a deep knowing that this was not aligned with us- but we kept going. Part of the process of deepening self-love is forgiving ourselves for those moments of self-betrayal and learning to honor our own powerful intuition. Intuition is often referred to as "knowing without knowing how we know."

Most often when we didn't follow our inner knowing, we were acting out on family trauma and patterns that may have kept us safe to a degree but didn't serve during those important moments. We live in a society that has not supported our intuitive development and instead has honored logical or group-mind decision making. It can feel scary to trust our inner knowing when others may not validate what we are perceiving. Trusting and following our intuition can lead us to aligned actions/decisions and to our purpose, better relationships and opportunities that truly inspire and expand our lives!

So how do we learn to honor our inner knowing in the face of all this? Find some time where you will not be disturbed and set up a journal, pen, candle and any crystals, images or comfy pillows that make you feel safe and peaceful.

1 Feel your feet on the ground and breathe deeply with eyes open. Take the candle and hold it in your hand and feel into what it would be like to trust yourself and receive inner guidance whenever you want! Light the candle and get comfy for this exploration.

2 Close your eyes, breathe deeply and allow your breath to flow into your belly. Repeat several times.

3 Breathe in the understanding that we are all intuitive and that our intuition shows up differently for each human being. Continue to repeat this understanding.

4 Another deep breath and review in your mind and heart a time where you had a strong intuition and you didn't listen- and then regretted it. As you remember, pay attention to how the information came to you? Was it a inner voice, hunch, knowing or feeling?

5 Release those images, now feeling into and remembering a time where you had an intuition, paid attention and made aligned decisions from that knowing. How did the knowing come through? Was it the same way as the time when you didn't listen.

6 Fill your body and heart with the remembering of the time you listened and now ask your inner knowing," What do I need to know right now?"

7 Pay attention and write down what you are receiving. It may not make sense right away or it might! In the coming days, you will continue to notice how your intuition communicates and recognize how listening and following it will bring you more into mind, body and spirit alignment and wellness!

8 Make a commitment to spend at least five minutes a day to breathe, center and allow your deep inner knowing to have the space it needs to support you into the best life and career/business!

REMEMBER, THE MORE YOU SHOW UP FOR YOUR AUTHENTIC TRUTH AND KNOWING, THE MORE ALIVE AND JOYFUL YOU WILL FEEL!

ABOUT VANESSA

Vanessa C. Codorniu is an acclaimed psychic medium with 25 years of experience and more than 10,000 individual sessions. She is a Bruja and Latinx teacher of intuition and clinical hypnosis, with a focus on healing ancestral trauma/patterns through hypnosis. A secret weapon for CEOs and entrepreneurs all around the U.S. and the Latin American world, Vanessa is most passionate about helping individuals develop their own inner resources, especially through intuition development and mindfulness tools.

Instagram @thebizbruja

Self-Love Ritual

WITH XTINA

You'll Need:

You (this one is most important)

Palo Santo/Sage/Copal

6, 15, or 24 crystals of a mixture of the following: Rose Quartz, Rhodochrosite, Rhodonite, and Clear Quartz

2 cups of Dead Sea salt or fragrance-free Epsom salt

1/2-1 cup of baking soda powder

6 drops of geranium/rose essential oil

Pink/Green/White candle(s)

Soft, soothing music

16 ounces of coconut/alkaline water

When feeling drained, overwhelmed, under-nurtured, anxious, stressed, heartbroken, cranky, or critical, try the following. Block out an hour for you and just for you, no interruptions, no excuses, no exceptions. If it applies, plan and inform your beloved that you are claiming a restorative and nurturing hour sans interruption. You can invite them to love you by supporting, honoring, and protecting this sacred time with/for you. Then unplug, disconnect, shut off, and initiate your gently powerful, loving focus on your self-love ritual.

Begin the Ritual

1 To start, clean the bathtub before you begin. It's always best to work with a clean, clear slate. Proceed to feel the tub with hot water, you can do lukewarm, and heat activates the cleaning properties of salt. It also helps to open the skin pores to let in all the water magic goodness.

2 As the tub fills, burn sage/palo santo or copal (use your intuition to choose which works best for you) and clear the bathroom. As you clear, call in source, the highest expression of love and light, and spirit guide assistance; set the space with your intention. Envision and invoke the feeling of your being an overflowing cup of juicy self-love.

3 Add in the Dead Sea/Epsom salt, baking soda, crystals, and essential oil(s). Bless the water with gratitude and invoke a personal blessing with each drop, i.e., "with gratitude to life source, may life nectar continue to be sweet and full of grace." Water has memory, and your crystals amplify your intentions.

4 Turn down the lights, love. Place and light your candle where you can see it. Put on soft, soothing music (be sure to keep your player/speakers in a safe place away from the possibility of water damage), disrobe, and submerge.

5 Allow your eyes to close and allow your body to surrender to the water's embrace. Inhale to the count of five. One. Two. Three. Four. Five.

And exhale to the count of five. One. Two. Three. Four. Five. With each exhale, visualize tree roots from your root chakra dropping down toward the center of the earth.

Repeat until you are fully present in your body.

6 To get present, bring your awareness and attention to the various sensations and feelings you are experiencing in your body in the present moment. Allow ALL senses the opportunity to feel, know, see, touch, taste, and hear. There is no need to adjust, fix, alter, suppress, or analyze. After acknowledging each sensation and feeling, allow yourself to let it go when you are ready.

7 Focus on your candle, soften your gaze, and shift your awareness above your head. Visualize a sun, moon, or both (let your intuition guide you here) with a steady stream of light flowing directly into your body. Let this light be the expression of compassion, love, and self-acceptance. Let it pour into the crown of your head and let it radiate down into your toes and roots. Feel it cleanse and relieve your body of tension.

8 When you are clearer and lighter, bring your awareness to your heart center. Visualize your inner child here. Ask how they are being. Connect and allow any thoughts, feelings, memories, and impressions to come through. Ask, "What do you need to feel loved today?"

9 Be curious. Stay open and receive.

WHEN YOU ARE CLEAR, COMMIT TO FULFILLING YOUR SELF-LOVE NEED COMPASSIONATELY.

10 Know you are worthy of being as you are, receiving loving action and grace. Shower your inner child with acceptance, quality time, attention, loving affirmation, service, kindness, and care.

11 Remember to stay hydrated throughout. It would be best to complete your water libation to hydrate and cleanse your body by the end of your bath. Use the rest of your quality time to enjoy and savor this gift. When done, you can journal about your findings and schedule your next self-love practice.

ENJOY!

ABOUT XTINA

Kristina Roman has 20 years' experience in body wisdom. She is a certified Sheila Kelly S-factor pole teacher in NYC, a Buti Yoga teacher, and trained energy healer.

Instagram @xrmvmnt

Vision Ritual

WITH YADI ALBA

"Becoming our Vision"

Becoming our Vision is our birthright, my Diosas, and all it takes is for us to recognize ourselves as powerful co-creators. Once we realize that we can transform our lives from the inside out by taking responsibility for all our beliefs- especially the ones sitting in our subconscious- we're well on our way.

Step 1

Reflect on what in your life you want to change. Give yourself permission to get real honest with yourself, pull out a journal and start jotting down all that is simply not working for you. Maybe it's a set of self-sabotaging patterns that you have outgrown, like not following through on those things that are most important to you or over extending yourself to others and leaving no time or energy for yourself. Maybe it's a problem in one particular area of your life that seems overwhelming and has been plaguing you for years such as an abusive relationship or a persistent health issue. Sometimes it can just feel like a subtle undercurrent of dissatisfaction that runs through all areas of our lives.

Step 2

Summarize your above reflections and place them in a list format. Now do your best to take an eagle-eye point of view as you observe your list and ask yourself, "What would a person who is co-creating all of these situations need to believe about themselves and the nature of life?"

Example:

-I hate my job.

-I'm alone and haven't found the love of my life.

-I don't have time to do the things that bring me joy.

A person co-creating these experiences may believe:

-I can't do what I love and make a living from it.

-True lasting romantic partnerships don't exist.

-I don't deserve to be happy.

Step 3

We are now transitioning to a very different part of this exercise where you are going to tune into the vision of your heart. It's important to note that we want to go inwards and so the vision will not be influenced by your fears and expectations or judgments of what you should be doing or being. This is where you get to whip out your magic wand that allows you to be bold and venture into the world of your imagination. With your magic wand, anything is possible, there is no room for limiting thoughts such as "but I'm too old for that", "but that would be so expensive", "but that's not realistic". Take your time answering these questions: If anything where possible, anything at all, what would I be doing with my life? How would I feel? How would I be of service to the world? What would my day-to-day look and feel like?

Step 4

Come back to your reflections of Step 3 and ask, "What would a person co creating that amazing life need to believe about themselves or the nature of life?"

Step 5

Congratulations, hermosa! You now know what beliefs are not serving you and what new beliefs you can start to re-inforce in order to change your life from the inside out!

ABOUT YADI

Yadi Alba is a modern day Medicine Woman, a vessel of ancient wisdom and a strong feminine force in our world. She brings spiritual principles into practical contemporary living. She's worked with countless celebrities and influencers, guiding them into the Embodiment of their Sacred Purpose. She is a published writer, master coach and has led workshops and retreats around the world.

Instagram @Yadi.alba

Shama Self-Love

WITH SHAMA DHANANI

SELF-LOVE TOOK ME INTO THE SHADOWS of what I've learned, what I've continued, and what I must release for space for my own personal reclamation of self-love, and the energy, time and resources I share. Self-empowerment and growth are not exclusive of self-accountability and responsibility, aka the ability to respond, which may come with more ease when there is harmony within inner and outer resources of mind, soul, body, and energy. I decided to take deeper action into self-love through repetitive practice, where it led me to more acceptance of self and others, sometimes in ways that meant being okay with letting go, always loving myself as a priority. I even lost thirty pounds during Covid with these consistent practices and the ripple of better decisions for my body.

My recent self-love journey centered on three consistent daily practices that took only a few minutes. The first practice is to write or speak three gratitude statements for self and three for others. Many days, it was gratitude for the willingness to be humble and listen, or the blessing of having reestablished a relationship with my father while I still can. Other days, it was a transmutation of harm and lessons learned into stronger roots and a wiser rise. A lot of days, it was for my new plants, and how they teach me to be patient, honor natural laws of growth and possibilities.

The second practice, also gratitude, focuses on body through embodied practices like dance, yoga, eating with nutrition at focus, and regularly looking at myself in the mirror, placing hands on my body, beginning at my heart, then letting it tell me where, and repeating "I love my body, and I love and honor myself daily in action."

The third practice is to focus on honoring the present in peace and co-creating by envisioning many possibilities during my morning meditations, knowing that the energy we create anchors our actions when we take the time to consciously co-create it in our minds and connect within the heart. The human mind operates in electrical currents, our heart in magnetic energy, just like Mother Earth. Harness the power that's already within, using a consistent practice as the anchor for programming new patterns for self-love. Meditation is the space our body, mind and heart - our nervous system - harmonizes. Let the thoughts go by, return to the heart of what brings happiness and peace to you, and from that place, envision all the possibilities you desire and willingness for even better. Every once in a while, take a look in the mirror and say to yourself, "It is so good to witness you rest, rise and live through conscious self-love."

WITH BLESSINGS,
SHAMA DHANANI

ABOUT SHAMA

Shama Dhanani is a Hypno Soul Coach & Trainer, Crystal Shaman & Meditation Teacher

Shama is a certified clinical hypnotherapist and trainer, spiritual advisor, meditation teacher and crystal shaman at www.ShamasLight.com. Shama's Light offers wellness seminars, private or group hypnotherapy and certification, chakra + mindfulness meditations, professional team building and workshops, and a web-based crystal, wellness and spiritual tools shop.

Email: Shama@ShamasLight.com; Instagram: @ShamasLight.com

A Self-Care Ritual to Fall in Love with You

WITH GIGI ROBINSON

MAKE TIME ON A FRIDAY NIGHT to give yourself praise and worship for the energy you constantly choose to give day after day. Create a healing bath with yellow flowers, dried rose petals, cinnamon, and some honey. I also add coconut milk to my bath, but if you have nut allergies, skip the coconut milk. While making your bath, say, "Thank you, I love you, you're doing GREAT work and you deserve love and self-care." As you soak, enjoy the sweetness and joy until you burst into laughter about the happiness you feel having everything you deserve. Feel how it would feel to be in that space right now and just stay there in the feelings of it.

When you exit your bath, stay in the vibration

Put on your gold (or yellow) things

Light green candles, then gaze into the mirror and tell God (or your ancestors) thank you for all the abundance that has opened up for you.

Affirmation you can speak:

I speak peace into my relationships with self and those that are nearest to me. May our light be a reflection of love that can be felt light years in time. May our actions only be expressions of who we are and what we are meant to be. May our love for one another be the token to a bountiful life, full of endless finances, endless love, and endless opportunities to expand into who WE are! I call on you, Mother Goddess, to reveal and release these blessings upon us all, that we may continue to reflect your fullness!

ABOUT GIGI

Living Aligned is the vision given to Gigi in January 2012 as a tool to navigate the transformation of her life and how she would share her process of Living Aligned and transparent with the world.

I AM Living Aligned combines the aspects of Intuitive Astrology (focus on emotional moon astrology), Life Activation Coaching and Waist Bead education.

Instagram: @IAMLIVINGALIGNED

JOURNAL PAGES

JOURNAL PAGES

JOURNAL PAGES

JOURNAL PAGES

JOURNAL PAGES

JOURNAL PAGES

JOURNAL PAGES

JOURNAL PAGES

JOURNAL PAGES

JOURNAL PAGES

JOURNAL PAGES

JOURNAL PAGES

JOURNAL PAGES

JOURNAL PAGES

JOURNAL PAGES

JOURNAL PAGES

JOURNAL PAGES

JOURNAL PAGES

JOURNAL PAGES

JOURNAL PAGES

JOURNAL PAGES

JOURNAL PAGES

JOURNAL PAGES

JOURNAL PAGES

JOURNAL PAGES

JOURNAL PAGES

JOURNAL PAGES

JOURNAL PAGES

JOURNAL PAGES

JOURNAL PAGES

JOURNAL PAGES

JOURNAL PAGES

JOURNAL PAGES

JOURNAL PAGES

JOURNAL PAGES

JOURNAL PAGES

JOURNAL PAGES

JOURNAL PAGES

JOURNAL PAGES

JOURNAL PAGES

JOURNAL PAGES

JOURNAL PAGES

JOURNAL PAGES

JOURNAL PAGES

JOURNAL PAGES

JOURNAL PAGES

JOURNAL PAGES

JOURNAL PAGES

JOURNAL PAGES

JOURNAL PAGES

JOURNAL PAGES

JOURNAL PAGES

JOURNAL PAGES

JOURNAL PAGES

JOURNAL PAGES

JOURNAL PAGES

JOURNAL PAGES

JOURNAL PAGES

JOURNAL PAGES

JOURNAL PAGES

JOURNAL PAGES

JOURNAL PAGES

Also Available

You can find **Goddess on the Go: Rituals to Help You Slow Down and Slay** at:

Amazon.com | BarnesAndNoble.com

Visit www.goddessonthego.com for other products and more information.

www.ingramcontent.com/pod-product-compliance
Lightning Source LLC
Chambersburg PA
CBHW062109080426
42734CB00012B/2804